Clockwise from top: Vegetable and Coconut Curry (page 71), Combination Nut Curry (page 71) and Spiced Potato Pancakes (page 76)

VEGETARIAN COOKING

Written & Compiled by
Jo Anne Calabria

Photography
Ray Joyce

Illustrations
James Gordon

MURDOCH BOOKS
Sydney • London • Vancouver

Simply Enjoyable Good Food

THIS EXCITING RECIPE book is not only for those committed to a vegetarian diet it's for anyone who enjoys good food and eating well. People from all walks of life are opening their minds (and mouths) to the exciting possibilities of vegetarian cooking.

Vegetarian Cooking offers simple, appetising and varied dishes from easy every day meals to entertaining for special occasions. We dispel the myth that "vegetarian cooking" is difficult and time consuming, and that "vegetarian food" is wholesome but heavy. We give you food that is fresh, seasonal, rich with variety and easily prepared. In our efforts to offer you the very best of this inspiring culinary world we have given you some recipes that include eggs and dairy products, if your interest lies with a strict vegetarian diet I urge you to seek the advice of a qualified dietition to help you achieve the best individual nutritional balance, use our recipes accordingly.

With todays extensive and abundant supply of fresh vegetables and fruit it makes it easy to plan your vegetarian menu around each season. Buy the best seasonal produce and choose your menu to complement the ingredients. Don't feel you must serve three courses when serving a vegetarian meal, take a lesson from our European friends and serve a selection of dishes alfresco style. Keep in mind the aesthetics of your menu, it should suit the season; light in summer, heartier in cooler months, add variety in texture, colour and flavour.

Keeping a well stocked store cupboard also makes it easy to prepare a wide range of vegetarian meals quickly and effortlessly. Having grains, rice, pasta, canned beans or lentils and a few other essentials on hand enables you to produce healthy, satisfying meals with a minimum of work and maximum effect. Add a few special flavour additions like a seasonal pesto or olive paste and you have the makings of a memorable meal.

The best thing about the recipes in this book is that they can be dressed up or down to suit the event; it may be a simple family dinner, a meal on the run for one or two, or a more formal affair. With each recipe we give you handy hints and tips for serving, substitutes for ingredients that are not readily available and valuable information about buying, storing and preparing the many vegetables and specific vegetarian ingredients used in our recipes. There are also step-by-step techniques and practical advice to help you achieve the best results.

Whether your enjoyment lies with cooking or you simply enjoy eating good food *Vegetarian Cooking* is for you.

JO ANNE CALABRIA

Front cover – Above: Apple and Camembert Tart (page 79). Below: Spinach Cheesecake (page 73)
Back cover – Above: Red Capsicum and Olive Salad (page 83). Below: Asparagus Bean and Pine Nut Salad (page 82)

CONTENTS

FOR YOUR CONVENIENCE WE HAVE USED THE FOLLOWING COOKERY RATINGS TO GRADE EACH RECIPE

COOKERY RATING:

easy   a little care needed   for confident cooks

Appetising
Starters & Soups

VEGETARIAN DISHES make an ideal start to any meal, they are generally light, wholesome and easily enjoyed. The delicious recipes for starters and soups in this chapter lend themselves to informal entertaining. Some, like the Potato Pancakes, Olive Paste and Fresh Vegetables or Polenta Antipasto can even be served as light meals with the addition of a salad, fruits and bread. We also give you rich, satisfying soups, try the quick and easy Fresh Bean Soup and for garlic lovers the Garlic Soup with Dumplings is a must. All the recipes we share with you in this collection are sure to make a special start to any meal.

Above: Olive Paste and Fresh Vegetables (page 8). Below: Potato Pancakes (page 8)

Deep-Fried Mushrooms with Sesame Soy Sauce

Mushrooms belong to the group of edible fungi. They are now readily and cheaply available most of the year thanks to modern growing conditions. Field mushrooms are only available at certain times of the year — mainly autumn — and have a stronger flavour. Mushrooms are graded into button, cap and flat. Always use mushrooms within 3–4 days after purchase. They must be stored in the refrigerator in paper or fabric — never in plastic as this will cause them to sweat. There is no need to wash mushrooms (which will make them too wet) — just wipe the caps with a damp cloth. Mushroom stalks can be frozen and used as a base for soups or vegetable stocks.

These mushrooms are encased in a light, crisp batter. The batter is made extra light due to the addition of a small amount of dried yeast and soda water. Do not wash the mushrooms — just wipe over with damp absorbent paper.

PREPARATION TIME: *45 minutes*
COOKING TIME: *10 minutes*
SERVES *4–6*

⅓ cup warm water
½ teaspoon dried yeast
½ cup plain flour
⅓ cup cornflour
2 teaspoons sesame seeds
½ cup soda water
1 egg white
24 small white mushrooms
oil, for deep-frying
SAUCE
½ cup soy sauce
½ teaspoon sesame oil
½ teaspoon grated ginger
shredded spring onion, for garnish

1 Combine warm water and dried yeast. Leave to stand for 10 minutes. Sift flour and cornflour into a basin. Mix in sesame seeds. Make a well in the centre of the dry ingredients. Gradually stir in the yeast mixture and soda water until the batter is smooth. Stand for 20 minutes in a warm place.
2 Place egg white into a clean glass mixer bowl and beat until soft peaks form. Gently fold egg white into yeast mixture.
3 Heat oil in deep fryer or large pan. Using a fork and spoon dip mushrooms into the batter. Cook in moderately hot oil until lightly golden. Drain on absorbent paper.
4 To prepare Sauce: Combine soy sauce, sesame oil and ginger in a small serving bowl.
5 Serve hot mushrooms on a plate, garnished with spring onion shreds and accompanied by sauce.

Olive Paste and Fresh Vegetables

A strongly flavoured paste made from black olives, good quality olive oil, fresh basil and lemon juice served with a platter of fresh, crisp vegetables is a perfect start to a meal. The olive paste can be made two–three days before needed.

PREPARATION TIME: *15 minutes*
COOKING TIME: *Nil*
SERVES *4–6*

500 g black olives
⅓ cup olive oil
2 cloves garlic, peeled
¼ cup basil leaves
1 tablespoon lemon juice
freshly ground pepper
fresh vegetables (snow peas, small radishes, pieces of cucumber, whole baby mushrooms)

1 Remove stones from olives. Place olives, olive oil, garlic, basil and lemon juice into the bowl of an electric blender or food processor.
2 Blend on high until the mixture is a coarse paste — do not over-process or the mixture will become too smooth. Season to taste with black pepper.
3 Serve paste in a bowl, surrounded by fresh, seasonal vegetables of your choice.

Potato Pancakes

Hot potato pancakes make a special start to a meal. Rinse grated potato in cold water to remove any discolouration.

PREPARATION TIME: *20 minutes*
COOKING TIME: *15 minutes*
SERVES *4–6*

4 large potatoes, peeled
3 eggs, lightly beaten

4 spring onions, finely sliced
3 tablespoons cornflour
2 tablespoons oat bran
oil, for frying
GARNISH
½ cup shredded spring onion,
grated fresh beetroot and
sour cream, to serve

1 Coarsely grate potatoes squeeze out excess moisture using your hands, and dry well in a tea-towel.
2 Place potatoes in a large bowl. Add eggs, spring onions, cornflour and oat bran. Mix well to combine.
3 Drop heaped tablespoons of the mixture into a well-oiled pan, flatten out slightly. Cook over a medium heat until pancakes are cooked through and golden brown on both sides. Drain on absorbent paper.
4 Serve hot, garnished with spring onion shreds or grated fresh beetroot and a dollop of sour cream.

Mushroom and Lentil Pâté

Serve this pâté as a starter at a dinner party accompanied by thin, crisp toast or crackers. The lentils must be very well-drained before combining them with the mushroom mixture.

PREPARATION TIME: *1 hour + chilling time*
COOKING TIME: *10 minutes*
SERVES 4–6

❧

1 cup yellow lentils
1 long strip lemon rind
1 bay leaf
60 g butter
1 onion, finely chopped
500 g mushrooms, finely chopped
1 tablespoon finely chopped oregano
1 tablespoon lemon juice
freshly ground pepper
fresh oregano leaves, for garnish

1 Place lentils, lemon rind and bay leaf into a pan and cover with cold water. Cover pan and simmer for 1 hour or until lentils are soft. Drain well.
2 Melt butter in a pan over a low heat. Add onion and cook for 1 minute. Add mushrooms, oregano, lemon juice and black pepper. Cook over a low heat until mushrooms are soft.
3 Combine well-drained lentils and mushroom mixture in the bowl of an electric blender or food processor and blend on high until the mixture is smooth.
4 Spoon mixture into one large or four-six individual serving bowls. Chill well before serving. Garnish with fresh oregano leaves.

When lemons are in abundance, squeeze them and store the juice in a bottle in the refrigerator for up to a week, or pour the juice into ice cube trays and freeze indefinitely. Add cubes of frozen juice as required to dishes while you cook.

Mushroom and Lentil Pâté

Fresh ginger is the root of a perennial plant that produces a strongly perfumed flower. Whole fresh ginger is readily available from most greengrocers. It is bought by the piece, often referred to as a 'hand' due to its shape. Fresh ginger should be smooth and free from blemishes with no obvious signs of withering or drying. Ginger is best kept in a cool, dry place away from direct light. For longer storage ginger can be peeled, placed in a plastic bag or small container and frozen. When needed, grate the required amount and return the unused portion to the freezer for future use. Another method of storage which some Asian people prefer is to peel the whole ginger and place in a screw-top jar, covered with dry sherry. Once the required amount is grated or chopped, the unused portion is returned to the sherry for future use.

Pesto and Ricotta Pizzas

These pizzas are a variation on the large Italian pizza, but still retain a true Italian flavour. A pesto sauce is used as the base, topped with ricotta cheese, and sun-dried tomatoes. Sun-dried tomatoes are available from many delicatessens. Wholemeal flour has been used for extra fibre and flavour.

PREPARATION TIME: *1 hour*
COOKING TIME: *15 minutes*
MAKES 6 *individual pizzas*

❧ ❧

PIZZA DOUGH
1 × 7 g sachet dry yeast
1¾ cups warm water
4 cups plain wholemeal flour
2 tablespoons olive oil
TOPPING
2 cloves garlic
1 cup fresh basil leaves
½ cup parsley sprigs
⅓ cup walnuts
¾ cup grated Parmesan cheese
½ cup olive oil
250 g ricotta cheese
250 g sun-dried tomatoes sliced

1 Combine yeast and water. Stand in a warm place for 10 minutes. Sift flour into a large basin. Make a well in the centre and add yeast mixture and oil. Mix well, using a wooden spoon, until dough forms a soft ball.
2 Knead dough on a lightly floured surface until it is smooth and springs back when touched. Transfer to a lightly oiled, large basin. Cover with plastic wrap and stand in a warm position until dough has doubled in bulk.
3 Prepare topping whilst dough is proving, by combining garlic, basil, parsley, walnuts and Parmesan in bowl of blender or food processor. Blend at medium speed, adding oil in a thin stream until a thick paste is formed.
4 Punch dough down and divide into six equal pieces. Shape each piece into a flat circle to fit the size of a saucer. Lay each piece of dough on a well-greased china saucer.

5 Spread each one with ricotta cheese, then top with the basil mixture. Arrange slices of sun-dried tomatoes on each one. Bake at 200°C for 15 minutes or until dough is golden brown and cooked through.
6 Remove pizza from saucer immediately and serve.

Ginger Tofu with Vegetables

Tofu is a product of soy bean. It is available at health food stores and Asian speciality stores. Choose firm tofu for this recipe.

PREPARATION TIME: *25 minutes*
COOKING TIME: *5 minutes*
SERVES 6

❧

½ cup light soy sauce
¼ teaspoon sesame oil
6, 5 × 5 cm squares firm tofu
1 teaspoon sugar
2 teaspoons grated ginger
½ cup white vinegar
2 carrots cut into 1 × 5 cm lengths
1 cucumber, peeled and deseeded cut into 1 × 5 cm lengths
1 tablespoon toasted sesame seeds

1 Combine soy sauce and sesame oil. Place tofu in a shallow dish and pour over soy mixture. Leave to stand at room temperature for 15 minutes.
2 Combine sugar, ginger and vinegar in a small pan. Stir over a low heat for 2 minutes. Put prepared vegetables into a bowl and pour over the vinegar mixture. Stand at room temperature for 10 minutes.
3 Place tofu onto an oiled tray and grill under medium heat for 3–4 minutes.
4 Serve a piece of tofu on each plate, accompanied by a serving of pickled vegetables. Sprinkle with sesame seeds.

Left: Pesto and Ricotta Pizzas. Right: Ginger Tofu with Vegetables.

Olive oil is produced from small green olives. The method for pressing olive oil varies from country to country and from region to region. Olive oil is like wine — it reflects the soil, the particular type of olive and the climate where that olive has been grown. Both the Italian and the Spanish olive oils are amongst the world's best. Pure virgin, first-pressed (cold-pressed) olive oil is the champagne of oils.

Cook cornmeal mixture over a low heat until thick, and it comes away from sides of pan.

Spread mixture evenly into a lined, greased Swiss roll tin. Refrigerate.

Polenta Antipasto

Cut polenta vertically then diagonally as shown, to form diamond shapes.

Polenta Antipasto

Polenta is yellow maize or cornmeal that is made into a thick porridge-like mixture and used in a variety of ways. In this dish it is topped with a selection of vegetables and cheese and grilled. Yellow cornmeal (maize flour) is available in supermarkets and delicatessens.

PREPARATION TIME: *45 minutes*
COOKING TIME: *3 minutes*
SERVES 4–6

3 cups vegetable stock or water
200 g yellow cornmeal
15 g butter
TOPPING
1 large red capsicum
8 small white mushrooms, sliced
1 zucchini, sliced
¼ cup olive oil
¼ cup red wine vinegar
125 g Cheddar cheese, grated

1 Pour stock or water into a pan and bring to the boil. Sprinkle in cornmeal, stirring until the mixture is combined. Reduce heat and simmer, stirring frequently for 15 minutes. The mixture should be thick enough to come away from the sides of the pan.

2 Remove cornmeal from heat and stir in butter. Brush a shallow 30 × 25 × 2 cm Swiss roll tin with oil. Line base and two sides with paper; grease paper. Spread cornmeal mixture evenly over tin. Refrigerate until needed.

3 Cut capsicum in half lengthways and remove the seeds. Place cut side down, under a hot griller and grill until the skin blackens and blisters. Remove from the griller and place into a plastic bag. Seal and leave 5 minutes. Remove capsicum from the plastic bag and peel off all blackened skin. Cut flesh into small squares.

4 Combine capsicum, mushrooms and zucchini in a basin. Add vinegar and oil. Mix well to combine.

5 Cut cornmeal into diamond shapes. Top each diamond with some capsicum, mushroom and zucchini. Sprinkle a small amount of grated cheese on top. Place on foil-lined griller and grill on high for 1–2 minutes or until cheese is melted. Serve immediately.

Coconut Pancakes filled with Sour Cream and Snow Pea Sprouts

Thin, delicate pancakes with a creamy sour cream, egg and snow pea sprout filling can be used to start a meal or as a light luncheon dish, accompanied with a green salad. Pancakes can be made the day before required. Cover and refrigerate, then bring them back to room temperature before using.

PREPARATION TIME: *35 minutes*
COOKING TIME: *20 minutes*
SERVES 4–6

1 cup rice flour
1½ cups coconut milk
1 egg
FILLING
2 small white onions, finely chopped
4 hard boiled eggs, chopped
1 cup light sour cream
1 × 250 g punnet snow pea sprouts
GARNISH
½ cup toasted shredded coconut
1 small red chilli, cut into fine shreds

1 Combine rice flour, coconut milk and egg to form a smooth batter.
2 Pour 2–3 tablespoons batter onto lightly greased crêpe pan, swirl evenly over base.
3 Cook over medium heat 1 minute or until underside is golden. Turn pancake over; cook other side. Transfer to plate; cover with tea-towel, keep warm.
4 Repeat process with remaining batter, greasing pan when necessary.
5 To assemble Pancakes: Fill each pancake with a spoonful of onion, eggs and sour cream. Top with a portion of snow pea sprouts. Roll and place onto warm serving dish. Spoon coconut and chilli down the centre of each pancake. Serve immediately.
Note: When choosing snow pea sprouts ensure that they are fresh, bright green, crisp and not slimy. Snow pea sprouts will keep in the refrigerator for 3–4 days. If snow pea sprouts are not available, substitute watercress.

Cottage Cheese Patties

These small, tasty morsels can be served as a start to any meal or as pre-dinner nibbles. Whatever way you serve them, they will be quickly consumed, especially if served with your favourite chutney, mayonnaise or dipping sauce.

PREPARATION TIME: *15 minutes*
COOKING TIME: *15 minutes*
SERVES 4–6

½ cup cottage cheese
2 spring onions, chopped
2 eggs, lightly beaten
3 tablespoons tomato paste
1 teaspoon Worcestershire sauce
1 cup brazil nuts, ground
2 slices wholegrain bread, crumbed
2 tablespoons chopped parsley
chutney, mayonnaise or sauce as a dip

1 Combine cottage cheese, spring onions, eggs, tomato paste, and Worcestershire sauce. Mix well. Add ground brazil nuts, breadcrumbs and parsley. Mix well to combine.
2 Divide mixture into twelve even portions. Form into patty shapes or balls. Deep or shallow-fry in moderately hot oil until golden brown. Drain on absorbent paper. Serve immediately.

Cottage cheese is a soft, unripened cheese made from skim milk. It is rich in protein and contains very little fat. It should be kept refrigerated at all times as it has a short shelf-life. Consequently, it should be purchased in small quantities.

Cottage Cheese Patties

Eggplant and Mozzarella Grill

Take some slices of wholegrain bread, coat them with a mixture of garlic and fresh basil, top them with slices of eggplant and mozzarella cheese, and grill them until the cheese has melted. A mouthwatering start to a meal or delicious accompaniment to any of our soups. The bread can be prepared a day before required and stored in airtight container.

PREPARATION TIME: *20 minutes*
COOKING TIME: *10 minutes*
SERVES 4

2 small eggplants
1 wholegrain French loaf
⅓ cup olive oil
3 cloves garlic, crushed
¼ cup finely chopped basil
8 slices mozzarella cheese
basil sprigs, for garnish

1 Cut each eggplant diagonally into eight slices, sprinkle with salt and leave to stand for 10 minutes. Cut French loaf also into eight slices on the diagonal.
2 Combine oil, garlic and basil. Using a glazing brush, lightly coat both sides of the bread slices with the mixture. Place bread on a baking tray and bake at 160°C for 10 minutes or until the toast is pale golden brown.
3 Rinse the eggplant and pat dry. Lightly brush eggplant with remaining oil mixture, grill on both sides until golden brown.
4 On each piece of bread, place a piece of eggplant, topped with a slice of cheese. Return to the griller and grill under medium heat until cheese is melted and golden brown.
5 Garnish each piece with a sprig of basil. Serve immediately.

Spinach Fritters with Walnut Sauce

In this dish, cooked spinach is combined with wholemeal breadcrumbs, eggs and Tabasco sauce, shaped into small patty shapes and shallow-fried. It is served with a yoghurt-based sauce. Tabasco is a hot pepper sauce made from fiery red peppers, so adjust amount to suit.

PREPARATION TIME: *20 minutes*
COOKING TIME: *6–8 minutes*
SERVES 6

12 spinach leaves, stalks removed
2 eggs
2 cups wholemeal breadcrumbs
1 cup walnuts, ground
4 drops Tabasco sauce
⅓ cup oil
SAUCE
½ cup toasted ground walnuts
1 cup plain yoghurt
pinch of ground saffron

1 Wash spinach under cold running water. Chop roughly and place in a pan. Cover and cook until the spinach is tender. Drain and cool. Using hands, squeeze spinach to remove excess moisture. Chop finely.
2 Put spinach in a basin, add lightly beaten eggs, breadcrumbs, ground walnuts and Tabasco sauce. Mix well to combine. Divide mixture into twelve equal portions. Shape each into rounds.
3 Heat oil in shallow pan. Add fritters and cook over a medium heat until the fritters are golden brown on both sides.
4 Whilst fritters are cooking, prepare the sauce by combining the ground walnuts, yoghurt and saffron. Stir well to mix.
5 Serve fritters with walnut sauce.
Note: If fresh spinach is not available substitute a 250 g packet of frozen spinach. To prepare frozen spinach for this recipe allow it to thaw then remove excess moisture by squeezing the spinach between absorbent paper. Tumeric is a good substitute for ground saffron, if unavailable.

Spinach can refer to both English spinach and silverbeet. Silverbeet is much larger, darker in colour and has a stronger and slightly bitter flavour. English spinach has smaller, paler leaves and a more delicate flavour. Both vegetables can be used in the same way. Both should be stored unwashed and wrapped in aluminium foil in the crisper section of refrigerator, or they can be placed stalk end down in a large jug of fresh cold water. Both must be well washed before cooking to remove grit. They can be cooked whole, chopped or shredded, in a minimal amount of liquid due to the vegetable's high water content.

Above: Spinach Fritters with Walnut Sauce. Below: Eggplant and Mozzarella Grill   15

Vegetable stock can be made by combining vegetables that will not overpower or cause the stock to become cloudy. Strongly flavoured vegetables to avoid are the turnip, swede and the cabbage family. Potatoes will cause the stock to become cloudy. Vegetables can be browned in a small quantity of oil before covering with water. This will produce a fuller flavoured, darker coloured stock. Stock is simmered until the vegetables are just tender. Strain and allow to cool before refrigerating or freezing. Freeze stock in usable amounts. Tomatoes may be added to the stock if a tomato base is required.

Fresh Bean Soup

Do not overcook the beans, otherwise the colour and flavour will be affected. Toast walnuts in the oven or under griller.

PREPARATION TIME: *25 minutes*
COOKING TIME: *20 minutes*
SERVES *4–6*

60 g butter
2 onions, chopped
2 cloves garlic, chopped
30 g plain flour
1 L vegetable stock
400 g fresh beans, topped, tailed, stings removed, cut into 2 cm pieces
2 teaspoons grated lemon rind
1 tablespoon lemon juice
2 tablespoons fresh oregano, chopped
½ cup roughly chopped walnuts, toasted

1 Melt butter in a large pan. Add onions and garlic and cook gently for 2–3 minutes without browning. Add flour, stir to combine and cook for 1 minute. Gradually add the stock. Stir until mixture boils and thickens slightly.
2 Add beans, lemon rind and juice, and oregano. Bring to the boil, reduce the heat and simmer, uncovered, until the beans are just tender. Remove soup from heat and leave to cool for 10 minutes.
3 Blend soup until smooth. Return to the pan and reheat gently.
4 Serve topped with toasted walnuts.
Note: If fresh beans are unavailable, frozen beans make a good substitute. This soup can be made ahead of time and kept in the refrigerator for up to 2 days. When ready to use gently reheat.

Spicy Lentil and Coconut Soup

A nutritious, easy-to-make soup that is spicy and just a little hot.

PREPARATION TIME: *20 minutes +*
15 minutes standing
COOKING TIME: *1 hour 5 minutes*
SERVES *4–6*

1 cup red lentils
1 tablespoon olive oil
1 clove garlic, finely chopped
1 onion, finely chopped
1 large green capsicum, finely chopped
2 teaspoons grated fresh ginger
1 teaspoon finely chopped red chilli
1 teaspoon garam masala
1 teaspoon ground cardamom
1 tablespoon chopped fresh coriander
2½ cups vegetable stock
2½ cups coconut milk
½ cup fresh coriander sprigs
½ cup chopped pimento

1 Cover lentils with boiling water and leave to soak for 15 minutes.
2 Heat oil in a large pan. Add garlic, onion, capsicum, ginger, chilli, spices and coriander. Cook gently 3–4 minutes.
3 Add drained lentils, stirring to combine. Pour in stock and bring to the boil. Reduce heat, cover and simmer for 20 minutes. Add coconut milk, stirring to combine. Continue to cook, covered, for 45 minutes.
4 Garnish with coriander sprigs and pimento.

Potato and Cheese Soup with Caraway Seed Toast

This thick potato soup is enriched by the addition of Gruyère cheese, though Swiss cheese could be used. Caraway Seed Toast is made using wholemeal Lebanese bread which is baked until it is a crisp dry wafer. Thinly sliced bread could be used in place of Lebanese bread.

PREPARATION TIME: *25 minutes*
COOKING TIME: *45 minutes*
SERVES *4–6*

6 large potatoes, peeled and diced
15 g butter
1 onion, finely chopped
2 tablespoons plain flour
2 cups low-fat milk
200 g Gruyère cheese, grated
1 tablespoon Worcestershire sauce
1 teaspoon French mustard

TOAST
2 large wholemeal Lebanese breads
¼ cup olive oil
1 tablespoon caraway seeds
fresh dill, for garnish

1 Place potatoes in a large pan and cover with cold water. Bring to the boil, reduce heat and simmer, uncovered, until potatoes are tender. Do not drain.

2 Melt butter in a large pan. Add onion and cook gently without colouring for 1 minute. Remove from heat. Stir in flour, then gradually add milk. Return to heat and stir constantly until the mixture boils and thickens. Add grated cheese, Worcestershire sauce and mustard. Stir well.

3 Combine potatoes, potato water and cheese-onion sauce. Stir well to combine. Return to a low heat. Simmer, covered, for 10 minutes.

4 To prepare Toast: Split each round of bread horizontally and cut each into six triangles. Brush with oil and sprinkle with caraway seeds. Bake at 160°C for 15 minutes or until crisp and dry.

5 Serve soup garnished with dill and accompanied by Caraway Seed Toast.

Left: Spicy Lentil and Coconut Soup. Right: Potato and Cheese Soup with Caraway Seed Toast.

Parsnip Soup

Always choose small parsnips as larger ones can often be woody in texture. Evaporated skim milk has been used to add creaminess.

PREPARATION TIME: *20 minutes*
COOKING TIME: *30 minutes*
SERVES 4–6

❧

60 g butter
1 kg small parsnips, peeled and chopped
2 onions, chopped
1 teaspoon curry powder
½ teaspoon ground cardamom
½ teaspoon ground turmeric
1 L vegetable stock
1 cup skim evaporated milk
croutons or chopped herbs, as garnish

1 Melt butter in a large pan. Add parsnips and onions. Cover and cook over low heat for 3–4 minutes.
2 Add curry powder, cardamom and turmeric. Stir to combine and cook for 1 minute. Pour in vegetable stock. Bring to the boil, reduce heat and simmer, covered, until vegetables are tender (about 30 minutes).
3 Remove soup from the heat. Allow to cool for 10 minutes. Blend in an electric blender or food processor until smooth. Return to pan. Add evaporated milk. Stir over low heat until soup is heated through. Serve with croutons or a sprinkling of fresh, chopped herbs.

The flavour of spices covers a wide range from hot through the aromatics to the sweet. Their uses are as unlimited as your imagination. To achieve the best flavour from any spice they should be heated before using either by cooking first in butter or oil or dry-frying in a small pan, but be careful as they can easily overcook and burn, causing a bitter unpleasant flavour.

Parsnip Soup

Garlic Soup with Dumplings

This is clear vegetable-based soup, enticingly flavoured with garlic, and each serving topped with a light dumpling. It is excellent served as a luncheon meal accompanied by Red Capsicum and Olive Salad (see page 83).

PREPARATION TIME: *30 minutes*
COOKING TIME: *1 hour*
SERVES 4–6

❧

2 tablespoons olive oil
8 cloves garlic, chopped
1 onion, chopped
2 stalks celery, chopped
2 carrots, chopped
1 L water
4 parsley stalks
1 sprig fresh thyme
2 bay leaves
2 tablespoons lemon juice
DUMPLINGS
1 cup plain flour
1 teaspoon baking powder
¼ teaspoon cayenne pepper
60 g butter
⅓ cup water or milk

1 Heat oil in a large pan. Add garlic and onion and cook until lightly golden. Add celery and carrots, and cook for 3 minutes. Add water, parsley stalks, thyme and bay leaves. Bring to the boil. Boil for 5 minutes. Reduce heat and simmer, covered, for 45 minutes.
2 Remove soup from heat and strain through a fine sieve. Return liquid to pan and heat slowly to simmering point. Add lemon juice.
3 To make Dumplings: Sift flour, baking powder and cayenne into a bowl. Rub in butter using the tips of your fingers. Make a well in the centre, add water or milk and mix with a knife until a soft dough is formed.
4 Place heaped teaspoonfuls of the dumpling mixture into the simmering soup. Cover and simmer for 15 minutes. Serve soup in individual bowls topped with one or two dumplings.
Note: Choose garlic bulbs that are compact, firm, plump and covered in a papery shell.

Clockwise from top: Walnut and Rosemary Scones (page 28), Garlic Soup with Dumplings and Fresh Bean Soup (page 16)   19

BASIC VEGETARIAN PANTRY

Having a store cupboard well stocked will make it easy to prepare a wide range of vegetarian meals quickly and effortlessly. You will need to spend a little time and effort to achieve a good working pantry, but the result will be worth it and all you'll need to do in the future is re-stock and replace what is used.

As a rule most wholefoods don't contain a lot of preservatives so it is a good idea to buy smaller quantities, remember the fresher the better. Choose the best quality and the brands you are familiar with.

Here are some ingredients to include in your basic store cupboard:

Mustard

Canned Tomatoes

Canned Capsicum Pieces

Tomato Paste

Dried Yeast

Eggs

Wild Rice

Short Grain Rice

Flour

Brown Sugar

Demerara Sugar

Vanilla Beans

BREADCRUMBS
Dry packaged crumbs.

CANNED GOODS
Canned goods are great standbys — keep a good supply of canned peeled tomatoes and pulses like lentils, chick peas, red kidney beans and so on on hand for quick and easy meals.

EGGS
Eggs are great for instant meals.

FLAVOURINGS
Stock up on soy sauce, tomato and chilli sauce, tomato paste, vegetable concentrates like stock cubes and miso (fermented soya bean), mustards and yeast extracts, they all add a powerful flavour boost to your dishes. Don't forget sweet flavourings like honey, maple syrup, brown and demerara sugar. Vanilla beans, essence or imitation vanilla essence are always useful.

FLOUR
Keep a small selection of wholemeal plain and self-raising, cornflour and baking powder are also useful for baking. Keep a small supply of dry active yeast for baking too.

GRAINS
As a general guide buy grains that are dry and plump and of a bright even colour, they should not have a musty or sour odour. Buy in small quantities and store them in airtight containers in a dry, dark cupboard. Some grains like brown rice, wholewheat grain and wheatgerm are best stored in airtight containers in the refrigerator. The following are the most popular grains:

Rice a popular grain and one of the best staple ingredients to have in the cupboard. Keep a selection of rice available, short grain rice is ideal for flavoured risotto and sweet dessert puddings. Long grain and the fragrant Basmati rice work well for pilaf recipes. Brown rice has a deliciously nutty flavour, it is available in short and long grain. The bran in brown rice offers extra protein, traces of iron, calcium and vitamin B, but takes longer to cook than white or polished rice. If rice, particularly brown rice is not used frequently then it is best to store in airtight container in the refrigerator.

Cracked and Wholewheat Grain are nutritious grains that are chewy, substantial additions to many dishes. Wholewheat grain has none of the germ or outer layers removed; it requires soaking prior to cooking and can be used as you would rice for pilaf dishes or simply cooked in vegetable stock and served as an accompaniment.

Cracked wheat is sometimes sold as kibbled wheat. This is the wholewheat grain that has been cracked between rollers, it cooks a little more quickly.

Burghul is cracked wheat that is hulled and parboiled, it is very popular as it requires little or no cooking.

Wheat flakes, wheatgerm and bran are the other variants of the wholewheat grain; all are available separately from good suppliers. They can be used in breads and baking and added to breakfast cereals.

Semolina is produced from the starchy part of the wheat grain, the endosperm. It is available from coarse to fine grain and can be used in pudding and cake making.

Couscous is fine semolina grain coated with flour, it is mostly steamed and served with spicy vegetable casseroles.

Cornmeal (made from corn) **and Polenta** (made from maize) are yellow to pale yellow, coarsely to finely textured. Their most popular use is for quick breads, muffins and baked polenta.

Barley Flakes, Rye Flakes, Oat Flakes and Rolled Oats are mostly used for home-made muesli and baking bread, they are also good to use as a coating for vegetable or lentil patties.

Pearl Barley is mostly added to soups and mixed with vegetables as a main or side dish.

Buckwheat and Roasted Buckwheat is generally used for pilaf-style recipes and as stuffings for vegetables.

HERBS

Fresh herbs are the best to use, but a small supply of dried herbs are always handy. Some useful dried herbs to have on hand would be oregano, thyme, bay leaves, dill leaves, basil leaves. Buy the dried variety in small quantities and store in airtight glass containers in a cool, dark place.

MILK

Dried powdered milk and long-life milk packets are good standbys.

Cream, coconut milk and coconut cream are also available in long-life packets all are easy and convenient to use.

Pearl Barley

Unprocessed Bran

Long-life Milk

Skim Evaporated Milk

Dried Dill Leaves

Rye Flakes

Rolled Oats

Dried Oregano Leaves

Buckwheat Kernels

Polenta

Dried Thyme Leaves

Semolina

Wheatgerm

Bay Leaves

NUTS

Small quantities of nuts are especially useful for adding instant goodness, crunch and flavour to many recipes. Almonds, walnuts, peanuts, pine nuts and pistachio nuts are good standbys. Use them whole or sliced, toasted or untoasted.

OIL

Olive oil and vegetable oil are essential cooking or salad oils for the store cupboard.

PULSES

Dried beans, peas and lentils make up the pulse family, keeping a range of different beans in the store cupboard enables you to produce a wide variety of healthy yet tasty dishes. When buying dried beans look for smooth whole beans without cracks or shriveled skins. Beans sold in bulk are often better than packaged beans. Most pulses will need soaking and cooking, exact time will depend on the type and quality of bean. Before cooking, pick over dried beans to remove small pebbles and any beans that are wrinkled or withered. Canned cooked beans and lentils are also good to have on hand to speed up preparation of some recipes. All pulses are a good source of dietary fibre, protein, iron, potassium and B vitamins. The following are just a few of the wide variety of pulses available:

Red Kidney Beans are particularly popular, they are kidney-shaped and deep red in colour. The red kidney beans are mostly used in soups, vegetable casseroles and salads. They can be used in place of pinto or borlotti beans.

Borlotti Beans are plump, slightly kidney shaped and beige to brown in colour with burgundy flecks. They are delicious mashed in dips and vegetable pâté.

Cannellini Beans are white kidney-shaped beans slightly squared off at the ends. They may be used in place of haricot beans. Ideal in soups and salads.

Pinto Beans are beige coloured and flecked with brown. Use as for borlotti beans.

Haricot Beans are small white oval-shaped beans that are used to make baked beans. They are delicious cooked and served in fresh tomato sauce.

Chick Peas are also known as garbanzos, they are round and rough textured with a pointed nib at one end. They are good in soups, stews, vegetable patties and dips.

Cashews

Chick Peas

Pine Nuts

Almonds

Cannellini Beans

Olive Oil

Walnuts

Vegetable Oil

Red Kidney Beans

Pinto Beans

Peanuts

Broad Beans are available dried, they range in colour from creamy to olive green to dark brown. They are a nutritious addition to any vegetable casserole and may be served puréed with cream as an accompaniment.

Black-eyed Beans, also called black-eyed peas, are small kidney-shaped beans, creamy white in colour with a black 'eye' on the skin, they are best when cooked, cooled and served with a dressing of olive oil and lemon juice.

Soy Bean are small beige coloured, very hard, oval beans. They can be used in place of haricot or cannellini beans.

Split Peas are split whole peas, they may be green or yellow. There is no need to soak split peas before cooking. They are excellent in soups and hearty stews.

Mung Beans are generally black or green and are most widely used for sprouting. The sprouted mung beans are a crunchy addition to salads and stir-fried vegetable dishes.

SEEDS
Seeds, such as sesame, poppy, pumpkin and sunflower seeds are ideal for baking (cakes and biscuits) and bread making. Store them in airtight glass containers in a cool, dry place.

SPICES
Spices such as ground or whole nutmeg, cinnamon sticks and ground cinnamon, ground ginger, sweet and hot paprika, cumin seeds, mustard seeds, ground chilli and pepper are all good to have in your store cupboard. They can be used to add flavour to savoury or sweet dishes, or for baking or pickling. Store in airtight glass containers in a cool dark place.

TOFU
Tofu or beancurd as it is sometimes called is available fresh and in long-life packets from Asian and health food stores. Some brands of long-life tofu will store for up to six months in your store cupboard. Silken tofu, dry tofu mix and tofu cheese are also available.

REFRIGERATOR STORE CUPBOARD
Small quantities of milk, yoghurt and buttermilk are invaluable to have on hand. Also keep small quantities of your favourite fresh cheeses and fresh tofu.

Yoghurt

Tofu

Black-eyed Beans

Sunflower Kernels

Red Lentils

Soy Beans

Brown Mustard Seeds

Cinnamon Sticks

Paprika

Whole Nutmeg

Sesame Seeds

Chilli Powder

Green Spilt Peas

Yellow Spilt Peas

Wholesome Breads & Baking

WE GIVE YOU our no-fail recipe for damper and an easy wholemeal bread recipe to make your own bread rolls, buns, knots or any shaped bread you like. Try the rich, Fruit Medley Loaf, serve it thickly sliced with lashings of butter, or the Savoury Pizza Snails and Walnut and Rosemary Scones with a thick hearty soup.

Your family and friends will certainly appreciate these home-made ideas.

Clockwise from top: Plaited Wholemeal Loaf (page 26), Pepita and Sunflower Seed Damper (page 26) and Pecan Soy Bread (page 32)

The humble potato has a long and interesting history. The Incas of Peru measured time by how long it took to cook a potato. The Irish potato blight caused widespread famine in Ireland during the middle 1800s. The potato in one form or another can be found in most cuisines of the world. There are several hundred varieties grown. Your greengrocer is the best guide when it comes to choosing the best potato for the purpose. Potatoes are one of the most adaptable vegetables, not to mention nutritious, economical and filling.

Pepita and Sunflower Seed Damper

This no-fail recipe for damper is guaranteed to be loved by all. Serve damper from the oven or spread with your favourite topping, be it cheese or fruit.

PREPARATION TIME: *10 minutes*
COOKING TIME: *40 minutes*
SERVES 6–8

⅓ cup pepitas
⅓ cup sunflower seeds
⅓ cup grated Parmesan cheese
pinch of cayenne powder
2½ cups wholemeal self-raising flour
1 cup buttermilk
1 tablespoon oil

1 Dust an oven tray lightly with flour.
2 Combine pepitas, sunflower seeds, cheese, cayenne pepper and sifted flour, including husks, into a large mixing bowl. Make a well in the centre. Add buttermilk and oil. Mix to a soft dough using a knife. Knead lightly and quickly into a ball. Turn onto a lightly floured surface and press into a 18 cm round.
3 Transfer the round onto prepared oven tray. Using a sharp knife, cut about 1 cm into the round, marking it into eight wedges. Sprinkle with extra Parmesan and pepitas if desired. Bake at 180°C for 40 minutes or until golden, crisp and cooked through.
Note: Pepitas are dried pumpkin seeds. They are green in colour and are available at some supermarkets and most health food shops.

Spicy Potato Rounds

Spicy Potato Rounds are very versatile — serve them hot or cold with tabbouli, grilled capsicum, hummus or eggplant dip.

PREPARATION TIME: *20 minutes*
COOKING TIME: *30 minutes*
MAKES *about 10 rounds*

2 cups mashed potato
1½ cups plain flour
¼ teaspoon ground turmeric
¼ teaspoon ground garam masala
1 teaspoon salt
½ teaspoon cumin seeds
2 tablespoons finely chopped coriander
1 clove garlic, crushed
¼ cup milk
60 g butter, melted

1 Place potato in a large mixing bowl. Sift flour and ground spices over potato. Add salt, cumin, coriander and garlic. Stir to combine. Make a well in the centre.
2 Add milk and melted butter. Stir with a knife to form a soft dough. Knead gently for 2 minutes until all ingredients are combined and the dough is smooth.
3 Roll dough between 2 sheets of plastic wrap or greaseproof paper to 1 cm thickness. Cut into rounds using a 10 cm plain biscuit cutter.
4 Arrange potato rounds on lightly floured oven trays about 3 cm apart. Bake at 200°C for 30 minutes, turning rounds over halfway during cooking time.

Plaited Wholemeal Loaf

Use this basic wholemeal bread recipe to make bread rolls, buns, knots, twists or any shaped bread of your choice. They will keep fresh in an airtight container for up to one week. To refresh bread, place it in hot oven for 10 minutes.

PREPARATION TIME: *1½ hours*
COOKING TIME: *45 minutes*
MAKES *1 plaited loaf*

1 × 7 g sachet dry yeast
2 tablespoons sugar
2½ cups wholemeal plain flour
1½ cups warm water
1¼ cups plain flour
½ cup wheatgerm
2 teaspoons salt
2 tablespoons oil
2 teaspoons milk (optional)
1 teaspoon sesame seeds (optional)

Spicy Potato Rounds

1 Combine yeast, sugar and half a cup of the wholemeal flour in a medium bowl. Gradually add water and blend until smooth. Stand, covered with plastic wrap, in a warm place for about 10 minutes or until mixture is foamy.

2 Sift remaining flours, including husks, into a large mixing bowl. Add wheatgerm and salt. Make a well in the centre, and add oil and yeast mixture. Using a knife, mix to soft dough.

3 Turn onto a lightly floured surface and knead for about 5 minutes or until the dough is smooth. Shape dough into a ball and place into a large, clean, lightly oiled bowl. Stand, covered with plastic wrap, in a warm place for about 30 minutes or until well-risen.

4 Knead dough again for about 3 minutes or until smooth. Divide dough into three equal pieces. Knead one portion at a time on lightly floured surface until smooth. Roll each piece into a long sausage of equal length, about 2 cm thick. Arrange lengths of dough side by side on flat surface. Press three ends together and plait towards opposite end. Press to seal ends together. Place on a lightly oiled oven tray. Cover with plastic wrap and stand in a warm place for about 30 minutes or until well-risen.

5 Brush with milk and sprinkle with sesame seeds if desired. Bake at 200°C for 25 minutes. Reduce heat to 180°C and bake a further 20 minutes or until well-browned and cooked through. Leave the plait on the tray for 5 minutes before turning onto a wire rack to cool.

Cheesy Mint and Sultana Ring

Your family or friends will appreciate this savoury cheese loaf on your next picnic.

PREPARATION TIME: *10 minutes*
COOKING TIME: *45 minutes*
SERVES 8–10

1¼ cups self-raising flour
1 teaspoon baking powder
¼ teaspoon ground cinnamon
1 tablespoon finely chopped mint
⅓ cup sultanas
2 cups grated Edam cheese
3 eggs
½ cup milk
2 tablespoons oil

1 Brush a deep 20 cm ring pan or a 20 cm baba pan with some melted butter or oil. Dust lightly with flour, shaking off any excess.
2 Sift flour, baking powder and cinnamon into a large mixing bowl. Add mint, sultanas and cheese. Make a well in the centre.
3 Beat eggs, milk and oil in small bowl with an electric mixer at medium speed for 3 minutes. Pour egg mixture into dry ingredients. Using a wooden spoon, stir until combined.
4 Spoon mixture into prepared pan and smooth surface. Bake at 180°C for 45 minutes or until a skewer comes out clean when inserted into the loaf. Stand in the pan 5 minutes before turning onto a wire rack to cool.

Capsicum Chilli Cornbread

Capsicum Chilli Cornbread is a tasty, slightly hot and nutritious bread suitable for the whole family.

PREPARATION TIME: *15 minutes*
COOKING TIME: *1 hour*
SERVES 6–8

2 cups fine ground polenta
2 cups self-raising flour
½ teaspoon ground chilli powder
1½ cups grated Cheddar cheese
½ cup finely chopped red capsicum
¼ cup pepitas
2 eggs, lightly beaten
2 tablespoons oil
1 cup soy milk
200 g carton natural yoghurt

1 Brush a deep 20 cm springform pan with melted butter or oil. Line the base and side with paper, and then grease paper.
2 Sift polenta, flour and chilli powder into a large mixing bowl. Add cheese, capsicum and pepitas. Stir well.
3 Make a well in the centre. Add eggs, oil, milk and yoghurt. Using a wooden spoon, stir until combined. Pour mixture into prepared pan. Smooth the surface. Bake at 180°C for 1 hour or until a skewer comes out clean when inserted. Remove from oven, and leave bread for 5 minutes before transferring it onto a wire rack to cool.

Walnut and Rosemary Scones

Scones are always popular. These scones have a subtle walnut and rosemary flavour. They are delicious served with a thick, hearty soup on a cold winter night.

PREPARATION TIME: *10 minutes*
COOKING TIME: *15 minutes*
MAKES *about 20 scones*

2⅓ cups wholemeal self-raising flour
⅓ cup oatbran flakes
60 g butter
½ cup finely chopped walnuts
3 teaspoons dried rosemary leaves
1 tablespoon currants
¾–1 cup milk
1 tablespoon milk, extra
1 teaspoon dried rosemary leaves, extra

1 Lightly dust an oven tray with flour.
2 Sift flour, including husks, into large

Poppy seeds are the tiny, blue-black seeds from the poppy plant. Although from the same family as the opium poppy, they do not have the same narcotic properties. The best poppy seeds are said to come from Holland. Poppy seeds are best roasted in a moderate oven (180°C) before using to bring out their full flavour. They are 50% oil so do not have a long shelf-life and are best stored in a sealed container in the refrigerator, so as to prevent them going rancid. They can be sprinkled over bread dough before baking, or used to thicken sauces. Some Indian recipes use them in curry dishes. Poppy-seed cake is a European delicacy.

mixing bowl. Stir in oatbran flakes. Rub butter into the dry ingredients using your fingertips, until the mixture resembles breadcrumbs.

3 Add walnuts, rosemary and currants. Make a well in the centre and add milk. Using a knife, mix to a soft dough.

4 Turn dough onto a lightly floured surface and knead until it is smooth. Flatten dough to 1.5 cm thickness. Cut into rounds using a 4 cm round or fluted biscuit or scone cutter. Arrange scones side by side on a prepared tray. Brush tops with extra milk and sprinkle with extra rosemary leaves. Bake at 200°C for 15 minutes or until puffed and golden.

Above: Capsicum Chilli Cornbread. Below: Cheesy Mint and Sultana Ring

Compressed yeast is best stored wrapped in greaseproof paper in the refrigerator. It will keep for up to a week, depending on its freshness. Freezing compressed yeast can destroy its rising qualities, especially if the yeast is not absolutely fresh. There is no way of telling how fresh compressed yeast is. It is best to buy only the required amount for each recipe.

Olive and Onion Focaccia

Focaccia is best when eaten hot, straight from the oven. The crisp exterior of this olive and onion focaccia gives way to its lighter, flavoured centre.

PREPARATION TIME: *1½ hours*
COOKING TIME: *45 minutes*
SERVES 6

❧❧

1 tablespoon olive oil
3 large onions, thinly sliced
30 g compressed yeast, crumbled
1 teaspoon sugar
3⅓ cups plain flour
1 cup warm water
2 teaspoons salt
⅓ cup olive oil
⅔ cup pitted black olives, coarsely chopped
1 teaspoon caraway seeds
2 teaspoons milk

1 Brush the base and sides of a shallow 19 × 29 cm baking tin with some oil. Set aside.
2 Heat oil in a pan. Add onions and cook over a medium heat for about 10 minutes or until soft and well-browned. Remove from the heat and leave to cool.
3 Combine yeast, sugar and a third of a cup of the flour in a medium bowl. Gradually add water, blending until smooth. Stand, covered with plastic wrap, in a warm place for about 10 minutes or until mixture is foamy.
4 Sift remaining flour and salt into a large mixing bowl. Make a well in the centre and add the oil and yeast mixture. Using a knife, mix to a soft dough.
5 Turn onto a lightly floured surface. Knead for about 5 minutes or until the dough is smooth. Shape dough into a ball and place in a large, clean, lightly oiled bowl. Stand, covered with plastic wrap, in a warm place for about 40 minutes or until well-risen.
6 Knead dough again for about 5 minutes or until smooth. Divide dough into two equal pieces. Roll out one portion of dough large enough to fit over the base of prepared pan. Press it down firmly into the corners. Spread two thirds of the cooked

onion over the dough. Top with two thirds of the olives. Sprinkle with half the caraway seeds. Roll out remaining dough to fit into the pan. Press dough firmly over filling and into corners.
7 Cover with plastic wrap. Stand in a warm place 15 minutes or until well risen.
8 Using a wooden spoon handle, make deep indentations randomly over the focaccia. Brush with milk and top with remaining onion, olives and caraway seeds. Bake at 200°C for 20 minutes. Reduce heat to 180°C and bake for a further 25 minutes or until well-browned, crisp and cooked through. Leave focaccia in the pan for 5 minutes before cutting and serving.

Quick and Easy Rye Bread Stick

Rye Bread Stick is best eaten on the day of baking. Serve sliced diagonally with thin shavings of fresh Parmesan cheese and sun-dried tomatoes.

PREPARATION TIME: *1 hour 15 minutes*
COOKING TIME: *35 minutes*
MAKES *1 loaf*

❧

30 g compressed yeast, crumbled
1 tablespoon molasses syrup
1 cup warm water
1¾ cups wholemeal plain flour
1½ cups rye flour
⅓ cup coarse rice bran
1 teaspoon cumin seeds (optional)
1 teaspoon salt
½ teaspoon sugar
2 tablespoons oil

1 Combine yeast, molasses and ¼ cup of the wholemeal flour in a medium bowl. Gradually add water and blend until smooth. Stand, covered with plastic wrap, in a warm place for about 10 minutes or until the mixture is foamy.
2 Sift remaining flours, including husks, into a large mixing bowl. Add the rice bran, cumin seeds, salt and sugar. Make a

It is crucial to remember when dissolving yeast, be it fresh or dry, that the liquid to be added is *lukewarm* and not hot or boiling. Hot or boiling water will destroy the yeast, and will prevent fermentation from taking place.

well in the centre and add oil and yeast mixture. Using a knife, mix to a soft dough.

3 Turn onto a lightly floured surface and knead for about 5 minutes or until the dough is smooth. Shape dough into a ball and place in a large, clean, lightly oiled bowl. Stand, covered with plastic wrap, in a warm place for about 30 minutes or until well-risen.

4 Knead dough again for about 3 minutes or until smooth. Shape dough into a log about 30 cm long. Place on a lightly floured oven tray. Stand covered with plastic wrap in a warm place for 15 minutes or until well-risen.

5 Using sharp scissors, make deep incisions along the top of bread stick at 2.5 cm intervals. Bake at 200°C for 20 minutes. Reduce heat to 180°C and bake a further 15 minutes or until well-browned and cooked through. Remove from oven, but leave bread stick on the tray for 5 minutes before turning onto a wire rack to cool.

Left: Olive and Onion Focaccia. Right: Quick and Easy Rye Bread Stick

Peanut Butter and Honey Scroll

Peanut Butter and Honey Scroll not only looks impressive but it tastes great too! It is best served warm while it is crisp and the flavour of the honey and peanut butter is at its peak.

PREPARATION TIME: *40 minutes +*
20 minutes standing
COOKING TIME: *45 minutes*
SERVES *6–8*

❧ ❧ ❧

2 cups plain flour
2 tablespoons oil
¾ cup water
⅓ cup smooth peanut butter
⅓ cup honey, warmed
⅓ cup rolled oats
⅓ cup chopped peanuts
2 teaspoons honey, extra
1 tablespoon rolled oats, extra

1 Brush a 20 cm round sandwich pan with some melted butter or oil. Line the base with greaseproof paper, then grease paper.
2 Sift flour into a large mixing bowl. Drizzle over oil, then rub oil into flour with your fingertips for 5 minutes. Make a well in the centre and add water. Using a knife, stir the flour into the water and mix to a soft dough. Knead dough in the bowl for about 5 minutes until smooth and elastic. Cover with plastic wrap and leave to stand for 20 minutes.
3 Cut dough in half, keeping one half covered. Roll one piece of dough to a circle 60 cm in diameter, and 1–2 mm thick. Spread dough with half the combined peanut butter and honey mixture right to the edges. Sprinkle with half the oats and half the peanuts.
4 Beginning at one side of the prepared dough, roll up tightly to the other side to form a long sausage shape. Carefully twist and stretch the sausage to resemble twisted rope. Roll into scroll and place in the centre of the prepared pan. Repeat the process with remaining dough and filling. Place the twisted rope around the first scroll to fill the pan.
5 Heat extra honey, brush over the scroll and sprinkle with extra oats. Bake at 180°C for 45 minutes or until crisp and golden brown. Leave to cool in pan.

Soya bean flour contains fat, protein and carbohydrate. It is a non-cereal flour suitable for diets that are low in protein and fat, such as that of the strict vegetarian.

Pecan Soy Bread

This slightly sweet and nutty flavoured bread will be favoured by all. Try shaping dough into individual sized dinner rolls, bows or knots for the children to enjoy.

PREPARATION TIME: *1½ hours*
COOKING TIME: *50 minutes*
MAKES *1 loaf*

❧

30 g compressed yeast, crumbled
⅓ cup golden syrup
¼ cup rye flour
¼ cup warm water
2¾ cups plain flour
½ cup soya flour
½ teaspoon ground cloves
½ teaspoon ground nutmeg
1 cup chopped pecan nuts
¾ cup soy milk

1 Brush the base and sides of 14 × 21 cm loaf pan with some melted butter or oil.
2 Combine yeast, syrup and rye flour in a medium bowl. Gradually add water and blend until smooth. Stand, covered with plastic wrap, in a warm place for about 10 minutes or until the mixture is foamy.
3 Sift flour and spices into large mixing bowl. Make a well in the centre, and add nuts, milk and yeast mixture. Using a knife, mix to a firm dough.
4 Turn onto a lightly floured surface and knead for about 5 minutes or until the dough is smooth. Shape dough into a ball and place into a large, clean, lightly oiled bowl. Stand, covered with plastic wrap, in a warm place for about 30 minutes or until well-risen.
5 Knead dough again for about 3 minutes or until smooth. Divide dough into three equal pieces. Knead one portion at a time on a lightly floured surface until smooth, and shape each into a ball. Arrange balls side by side in the prepared pan. Cover with plastic wrap, stand in a warm place for 30 minutes or until well-risen.
6 Bake loaf at 200°C for 25 minutes. Reduce heat to moderate and bake a further 25 minutes or until well-browned, and cooked through. Leave loaf in pan for 5 minutes before turning onto a wire rack.

Above: Peanut Butter and Honey Scroll. Below: Savoury Pizza Snails (page 35)

Continental Wholemeal Bread

Try this tasty bread on its own or serve it with a thick vegetable casserole or vegetable curry. It is also delicious spread with fruit chutney and yoghurt.

PREPARATION TIME: *10 minutes*
COOKING TIME: *25 minutes*
SERVES 6

Rice flour, potato flour and cornflour are often used in recipes to give a lighter, finer texture to breads, cakes, pastries and biscuits. They also make great thickening agents in sauces, soups and custards.

1½ cups plain wholemeal flour
½ cup self-raising flour
⅓ cup pine nuts
⅓ cup chopped flat-leaved parsley
2 teaspoons dried sweet basil leaves
1 clove garlic, crushed
2 teaspoons sugar
2 eggs lightly beaten
¾ cup milk
1 tablespoon oil

1 Brush a shallow 19 × 29 cm baking pan with melted butter or oil. Line the base and sides with paper and then grease the paper.
2 Sift flours, including husks, into a large mixing bowl. Add nuts, parsley, basil, garlic and sugar. Stir to combine.
3 Make a well in the centre. Combine eggs, milk and oil, and pour into the bowl. Stir with a wooden spoon until combined.
4 Pour mixture into the prepared pan. Smooth the surface. Bake at 180°C for 25 minutes or until golden and cooked through. Turn onto a wire rack to cool.

Continental Wholemeal Bread

Sesame Pepper Crispbreads

Sesame pepper crispbreads will keep stored in an airtight container for up to two weeks. Eat them as they are, or spread with ricotta cheese and avocado. They are great for lunch or eaten as a snack.

PREPARATION TIME: *5 minutes*
COOKING TIME: *45 minutes*
MAKES *about 40 crispbreads*

2 egg whites
⅓ cup caster sugar
½ cup sunflower seeds
⅔ cup sesame seeds
1½ teaspoons cracked black peppercorns
2 tablespoons tahini paste
⅔ cup wholemeal plain flour

1 Brush an 8 × 26 cm log pan with melted butter or oil. Line the base and sides with paper and then grease paper.
2 Beat egg whites in a small bowl with an electric mixer until stiff peaks form. Add sugar gradually, beating well after each addition. The mixture should resemble consistency of meringue.
3 Transfer the mixture to a large mixing bowl. Add the sesame seeds, peppercorns, tahini paste and sifted flour, including husks. Using a metal spoon, fold all ingredients together until combined.
4 Spoon mixture into prepared pan, pressing firmly into corners. Smooth the surface. Bake at 180°C for 30 minutes or until just golden. Remove from oven. Turn onto a wire rack to cool.
5 Using a serrated edged knife, cut bread into 5 mm thick slices. Arrange slices side by side on ungreased oven trays, bake at 180°C a further 10–15 minutes or until golden and crisp. Cool on trays.
Note: Tahini paste is made from ground toasted sesame seeds which make a smooth creamy-grey coloured paste. Its flavour is nutty and slightly bitter. Tahini paste is available in health food shops, Middle Eastern or Greek speciality shops and will keep for up to 6 months sealed and stored in the refrigerator. Tahini separates on standing so stir well before using.

Savoury Pizza Snails

Serve Savoury Pizza Snails at your next birthday party, cocktail party or pack them for lunch. They are delightfully tasty hot or cold and are a great accompaniment to soups and casseroles.

PREPARATION TIME: *1 hour*
COOKING TIME: *30 minutes*
MAKES *about 35*

1 tablespoon olive oil
1 onion, finely chopped
½ cup finely chopped green capsicum
¼ cup finely chopped black olives
30 g compressed yeast, crumbled
1 teaspoon sugar
½ cup wholemeal plain flour
1¼ cups warm water
2¼ cups plain flour
½ cup rye flour
1 teaspoon salt
¼ cup tomato paste
2 teaspoons dried sweet basil leaves
1 cup grated Cheddar cheese

1 Heat oil in a pan. Add onion and capsicum and cook over a low heat for about 8 minutes or until soft. Add olives to pan and cook for 2 minutes. Remove from heat and leave to cool.
2 Combine yeast with sugar and wholemeal flour in a medium bowl. Gradually add water and blend until smooth. Stand, covered with plastic wrap, in a warm place for about 10 minutes or until mixture is foamy.
3 Sift remaining flours into a large mixing bowl and add salt. Make a well in the centre and add yeast mixture. Using a knife, mix to a soft dough.
4 Turn onto a lightly floured surface. Knead for about 5 minutes or until the dough is smooth. Shape dough into a ball and place into a large, clean, lightly oiled bowl, stand, covered with plastic wrap, in a warm place for about 30 minutes or until well-risen.
5 Knead dough again for about 3 minutes or until smooth. Roll dough out on a lightly floured surface to a 30 × 45 cm rectangle. Spread evenly with tomato paste. Top with cooled vegetable mixture. Sprinkle with basil and cheese.

Roll dough out on a lightly floured surface to a 30 × 45 cm rectangle.

Spread dough evenly with tomato paste, sprinkle with cooled vegetable mixture.

Roll dough up tightly. Using a sharp knife, cut through roll to base.

6 Roll up tightly along the widest part of the dough to the other side. Using a sharp knife, cut through roll to base at 1 cm intervals. Arrange 'snails' on lightly oiled tray about 8 cm apart. Cover with plastic wrap, stand in a warm place for 20 minutes or until well-risen.
7 Bake at 200°C for 15 minutes. Reduce heat to 180°C and bake a further 15 minutes or until golden and crisp. Leave snails on trays for 5 minutes before transferring to a wire rack to cool.

The onion family boasts an impressive list of varieties, which are used in some form or another in most of the world's savoury dishes. They vary in flavour and heat, from the very mild, red, Spanish onion which can be eaten raw (they are ideal for salads), to the strong, pungent, brown onion which is best cooked to develop its natural sweetness. Also in the onion family are spring onions, shallots, leeks and, of course, garlic — all of which have their own special place in many cuisines.

Fruit Medley Loaf

You can't beat homemade fruit loaf. Eat it warm, or serve it cold spread with butter or cottage cheese. Fruit Medley Loaf can be sliced and toasted successfully for breakfast or brunch.

PREPARATION TIME: *1½ hours*
COOKING TIME: *40 minutes*
MAKES *1 loaf*

Stand yeast mixture in a warm place for about 10 minutes or until foamy.

When a recipe requires finely chopped dried fruits, snip each fruit with sharp kitchen scissors to the desired fineness, or process them in a food processor using the pulse action of your machine.

30 g compressed yeast, crumbled
1 tablespoon brown sugar
1¼ cups warm water
2¼ cups plain wholemeal flour
1¼ cups plain flour
2 teaspoons mixed spice
1 teaspoon salt
1½ cups dried mixed fruit
1 tablespoon malt extract
1 tablespoon oil

Sift flour and spice into bowl, add fruit, malt extract, oil and yeast mixture.

Dried fruit is nourishing, and rich in vitamins and minerals. If you are suffering from a lack of iron, some dried fruits can help to restore this mineral to your diet — the best being figs and peaches, then prunes and raisins. Choose the best quality plump fruit which can be eaten straight from the packet. They can also be soaked in water for a short time to 'plump' them before eating.

1 Brush the base and sides of 15 × 25 cm loaf pan with melted butter or oil.
2 Combine yeast, sugar and quarter cup of the plain flour in a medium bowl. Gradually add water and blend until smooth. Stand, covered with plastic wrap, in a warm place for about 10 minutes or until the mixture is foamy.
3 Sift remaining flours, including husks, spice and salt into large mixing bowl. Make a well in centre, add fruit, malt extract, oil and yeast mixture. Using a knife, mix to a firm dough.
4 Turn onto a lightly floured surface and knead for about 3 minutes or until dough is smooth. Shape dough into a ball, place into a large, clean, lightly oiled bowl. Stand, covered with plastic wrap, in a warm place for about 40 minutes.
5 Knead dough again for about 2 minutes or until smooth. Divide dough into two equal portions. Knead one portion on a lightly floured surface for 2 minutes. Shape into ball. Repeat with remaining dough. Arrange balls side by side in the prepared pan. Cover with plastic wrap, stand in a warm place for 30 minutes or until well-risen.
6 Bake loaf at 200°C for 40 minutes or until well-browned and cooked through. Leave the loaf in the pan for 5 minutes before turning out onto a wire rack.

Knead dough on a lightly floured surface for about 3 minutes or until smooth.

Shape each portion of dough into a ball, arrange side by side in a prepared pan.

Above: Fruit Medley Loaf. Below: Sesame Pepper Crispbreads (page 34)

TECHNIQUES FOR VEGETARIAN ESSENTIALS

With these step-by-step guidelines we show you how to master the techniques that are necessary to produce some of the essential vegetarian ingredients.

VEGETABLE STOCK

Whatever soup, stew or pasta dish you are making it will certainly be enhanced by a rich vegetable stock. A good all purpose vegetable stock can be used in place of water or other liquids in vegetarian recipes, providing added flavour.

There are some essential points to follow when making a vegetable stock, firstly choose the freshest ingredients for the best results, use onions, leeks, carrots, celery, parsley and other fresh herbs. It is best not to use starchy vegetables like potatoes or pumpkin as they produce a cloudy stock (they are fine for creamy potato soup etc) and vegetables like cabbage and spinach are too strong in flavour and colour.

1 To make 2 litres of stock you will need about 500 g of uncooked vegetables. Wash all vegetables thoroughly before making stock.

2 Vegetable stock needs only a short cooking time, 40 minutes of slow, gentle simmering is all it takes to release the essential flavours. Any longer and the vegetables begin to disintegrate and cloud the stock.

3 Add a bouquet garni to the stock to add flavour, coarse salt or black peppercorns may be added also, avoid using ground pepper as long slow simmering of ground pepper gives a sharp after taste.

4 Strain the stock immediately after cooking, take care when straining so as not to disturb vegetables to avoid clouding. If you want a more concentrated flavour boil the strained stock slowly until it reaches the required strength.

Store stock covered in the refrigerator for up to two days, or freeze for up to two months.

Vegetable stock needs only a short cooking time, 40 minutes gentle simmering over a low heat is best.

Add a bouquet garni of celery, bay leaves, parsley and herbs as well as an onion studded with cloves.

Carefully strain the stock immediately after cooking, this avoids clouding the stock.

FRESH TOMATO SAUCE

A flavoursome tomato sauce is a great standby to have on hand in any kitchen, it can be used to dress hot and cold pasta dishes, as a light accompaniment to vegetable pies, roulades, crêpes and terrines. Make the most of ripe red seasonal tomatoes they have the best flavour and colour. The foundation of a good tomato sauce lies with the cooking, light short cooking produces a light, fragrant sauce and low slow simmering gives a rich full bodied sauce.

1 To make 3 cups of tomato sauce you will need about 1 kg of ripe, peeled tomatoes.

2 Cook a finely chopped white onion in a small amount of olive oil, add two stalks of finely chopped celery, cook stirring until soft.

3 Reduce heat and add the peeled tomatoes and one cup of vegetable stock or red wine and a pinch of sugar, simmer uncovered stirring often for about 30 minutes or until sauce is thick.

4 Season lightly with finely chopped basil, dried oregano and a little salt and pepper, if desired. A drizzle of olive oil also adds richness. This sauce can be used immediately, it can also be stored, covered for up to three days in the refrigerator or the sauce can be successfully frozen for up to three months.

Cook *chopped onion and celery in olive oil over a low heat until vegetables are soft, but not golden.*

Add *the ripe, peeled tomatoes to pan, add the vegetable stock or red wine, mix well.*

Simmer *tomato mixture uncovered, stirring often for about 30 minutes until sauce is thick.*

SPROUTING

Sprouts from seeds, beans and grains are a great source of nutritional value in any diet but especially useful in the vegetarian diet. All are rich in vitamins C, A, B1, B2 and D. Sprouts of many varieties are available fresh from the greengrocers. Sprouts can also be very easily grown in your own kitchen.

1 Purchase the beans, seeds or grains of your choice. Use ¼ to ½ cup of seeds depending on the size of your container which can be a clean sterilised jar or a purchased sprouting container.

2 Rinse the seeds in clean, cold water, then place them in your chosen containers.

3 Cover with some fresh cold water and leave to soak for 12 to 24 hours.

4 Drain away water, cover the mouth of the jar with cheesecloth or muslin.

5 Turn the jar on it's side to drain and place in a cool, dark place for 12 hours. Remove the container to a light, but not directly sunlit place.

6 Rinse and drain the sprouts every day for three to four days or until seeds begin to sprout. Sprouts should be ready to use when they are 2.5 to 3 cm in length and bright green in colour. Store sprouts in refrigerator, use them within two days.

Place *beans or seeds in sterilised container, cover with water.*

Rinse *and drain the sprouts daily with water for three or four days.*

After *four days the sprouts should be ready to use.*

Easy Pasta, Rice & Grain Dishes

PASTA, RICE AND GRAINS are an important source of inspiration in the vegetarian diet, they are all very versatile, teamed with a few other essential ingredients they enable the vegetarian cook to produce quick and easy meals with a minimum of effort and with maximum effect.

As a general rule wholefood products, like wholemeal pasta, rice and grains have little preservatives, so it is best to buy smaller quantities and replace when needed. Cook pasta, rice and grains in a large pan of rapidly boiling water, unless otherwise stated in the recipe. Cook only until just tender.

In this inspirational collection we give you Pasta with Coriander Pesto, Fragrant Rice and Lentils, Citrus Risotto and Barley and Mushroom Bake and many more that all the family will love.

Above: Fragrant Rice and Lentils (page 42). Below: Pasta with Coriander Pesto (page 42)

Tagliatelle in Cream Sauce

Cottage cheese has been used to produce this thick, creamy sauce that coats the tagliatelle beautifully. Any ribbon pasta may be used in place of tagliatelle.

PREPARATION TIME: *10 minutes*
COOKING TIME: *10 minutes*
SERVES 4–6

500 g dried wholemeal tagliatelle
30 g butter
2 onions, finely chopped
250 g creamed cottage cheese
2 tablespoons cream
½ cup freshly grated Parmesan cheese
freshly grated pepper
¼ cup sliced green, pimento stuffed olives

1 Cook tagliatelle in a large quantity of boiling water until just cooked.
2 While pasta is cooking, melt butter over a low heat. Add onion and cook for 3–4 minutes until onion is soft. Do not brown. Stir in cottage cheese and cream. Cook over a low heat until the cheese has melted and is heated through. Add Parmesan and pepper. Stir to combine.
3 Drain tagliatelle. Place in a large bowl and add sauce. Toss to combine. Top with sliced olives, and serve immediately.

While cooking pasta add a peeled clove of garlic to the water, but do remember to remove it before serving pasta.
Add a citrus tang to pasta or noodles by adding strips of orange or lemon peel to water while cooking, remove before serving.

Tagliatelle in Cream Sauce

Pasta with Coriander Pesto

Pesto is a cold sauce of Italian origin which is made using fresh basil. This version is made using coriander which produces a strong aromatic sauce that tastes wonderful with pasta.

PREPARATION TIME: *15 minutes*
COOKING TIME: *12 minutes*
SERVES 4–6

500 g dried spinach fettuccine
1 bunch coriander
¾ cup olive oil
¼ cup pine nuts
1 clove garlic, peeled
½ cup freshly grated Parmesan cheese
2 tablespoons poppy seeds
extra toasted pine nuts, to garnish

1 Cook pasta in a large quantity of boiling water until just tender.
2 While the pasta is cooking, wash coriander well under cold running water. Cut away root end of coriander and discard. Roughly chop stems and leaves. Blend coriander, olive oil, pine nuts and garlic in a blender or food processor until mixture is well combined.
3 Transfer coriander mixture to a bowl. Stir in Parmesan cheese and poppy seeds.
4 Drain hot fettuccine and mix through pesto mixture. Place on a large serving platter, sprinkle with extra toasted pine nuts.

Fragrant Rice and Lentils

Fragrant spices from the East combine with brown rice and lentils to produce this interesting and tasty main course dish.

PREPARATION TIME: *15 minutes*
COOKING TIME: *45 minutes*
SERVES 4–6

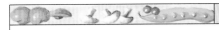

1 tablespoon olive oil
1 onion, finely chopped
1 teaspoon turmeric
¼ teaspoon cardamom seeds
¼ teaspoon ground cinnamon
1 teaspoon garam masala
1 teaspoon ground cardamom
1 teaspoon brown mustard seeds
2 cinnamon sticks
2 cups brown rice
1 cup brown lentils
5 cups water
4 hard-boiled eggs
½ cup almonds, toasted
½ cup Brazil nuts, toasted

1 Heat oil in a large pan. Add onion and cook over a low heat until golden brown. Add spices, mustard seeds and cinnamon sticks and cook for a minute, stirring continuously, to release aroma.

2 Add rice and lentils, stirring to combine. Pour in water and bring to the boil. Reduce to a low heat and simmer, covered, for 40 minutes or until rice and lentils are tender. Stir through eggs and toasted nuts.

Pasta with Broccoli and Spinach

Simply delicious are the best words to describe this pasta dish. Tender cooked penne topped with broccoli and spinach, simmered in nutmeg and white wine, coated with melted Parmesan and Cheddar cheese, produces a tasty, satisfying meal.

PREPARATION TIME: *25 minutes*
COOKING TIME: *5 minutes*
SERVES 4–6

400 g penne pasta
30 g butter
1 onion, chopped
½ teaspoon ground nutmeg
250 g broccoli cut into florets
½ cup white wine
6 spinach leaves, shredded
½ cup freshly grated Parmesan cheese
½ cup grated Cheddar cheese

1 Cook pasta in a large quantity of boiling water until just tender. Drain and place in a greased, shallow, ovenproof dish, keep warm.

2 Melt butter in a large pan. Add onion and cook over a low heat for 3–4 minutes. Add nutmeg, broccoli and spinach. Pour over wine. Cover and cook over low heat for 5 minutes.

3 Spoon vegetable mixture over pasta. Top with cheeses. Bake at 180°C for 5 minutes or until cheese has melted and browned. Serve immediately accompanied by green salad.

Pasta with Broccoli and Spinach

Coconut milk and coconut cream can be purchased in cans and cartons in most supermarkets. It can also be made very easily be using desiccated coconut and milk. To produce 1 cup of coconut milk, combine 1½ cups coconut and 1½ cups milk in a small saucepan. Simmer over a low heat, stirring once or twice for 3–4 minutes. Cool until room temperature. Strain through a fine strainer, pressing the coconut well to extract all the coconut milk. Cool and use as required. If you require coconut cream, chill the milk and then skim the cream from the top. Coconut milk and cream can be stored in the refrigerator for 3–4 days.

Make well in centre of flour, add eggs, gradually incorporate flour with fork.

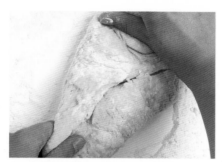

As mixture begins to form a ball, turn onto a lightly floured surface and knead.

Knead dough until smooth and elastic, continue kneading for about 10 minutes.

To make noodles: Roll up pasta sheet, cut with a sharp knife into 5 mm wide strips.

Oriental Noodles with Chilli and Cashews

Cashew paste is available at most health food stores.

PREPARATION TIME: *25 minutes +*
30 minutes standing
COOKING TIME: *10 minutes*
SERVES 6

2½ cups plain flour
pinch salt
4 eggs, lightly beaten
1 egg for glazing, lightly beaten
SAUCE
1 teaspoon vegetable oil
1 small red chilli, finely chopped
1 spring onion, finely chopped
250 g snow peas, thinly sliced
½ teaspoon sesame oil
¼ cup light soy sauce
½ cup malt vinegar
¼ cup cashew paste
1 tablespoon lime juice
1 teaspoon finely grated lime rind
1 red chilli, finely shredded (extra)
½ cup lightly roasted cashews

1 To make Noodles: Sift flour and salt into a bowl. Make a well in the centre and add the beaten eggs, gradually incorporate into flour with a fork. Turn onto a lightly floured surface and knead until smooth and elastic, about 5 minutes. Cover and stand for 30 minutes.
2 Divide dough into four portions. Cover with a tea-towel. Roll one portion of dough to 3 mm thickness, using rolling pin or pasta machine or sharp knife. Roll up the sheet of pasta completely, cut pasta into 5 mm wide strips. Carefully unroll strands. Repeat process with remaining portions of dough. Spread onto dry tea-towel, sprinkle with plain flour; set aside.
3 Prepare sauce whilst the pasta is standing. Heat oil in a pan, then add chilli and spring onion and snow peas. Cook over a low heat for 2–3 minutes. Add sesame oil, soy sauce, vinegar, cashew paste, lime juice and rind. Stir to combine. Cook, stirring, over a gentle heat 3–4 minutes.
4 Cook pasta in a large quantity of boiling water until just tender. Drain. Spoon over sauce and toss to combine. Sprinkle over shredded chilli, cashews and serve.

Above: Crisp Fried Noodles and Chilli Vegetables (page 46). Below: Oriental Noodles with Chilli and Cashews.   45

Barley and Mushroom Bake

Barley and Mushroom Bake

Not only is barley high in fibre but it has a wonderful nutty flavour and chewy texture. This recipe is great served as a winter luncheon meal.

PREPARATION TIME: *20 minutes*
COOKING TIME: *55 minutes*
SERVES 4–6

1 tablespoon olive oil
2 onions, chopped
1 red capsicum, chopped
1½ cups pearl barley
2 cups vegetable stock
125 g button mushrooms
1 cup light sour cream
1 × 25 g packet plain corn chips
1 cup grated low-fat Cheddar cheese

1 Heat oil in a pan. Add onion and capsicum and cook over a gentle heat 3–4 minutes. Add barley and stir over a low heat for 3–4 minutes. Add stock, cover and bring to the boil. Reduce heat and simmer, uncovered for 40 minutes. Add mushrooms and cook for a further 5 minutes.
2 Place barley mixture into lightly greased, ovenproof dish. Spoon over sour cream. Top with corn chips and sprinkle with cheese. Bake at 180°C for 10 minutes.

Crisp Fried Noodles and Chilli Vegetables

An Asian-style vegetable dish that can be served alone or as part of a full meal. Chinese vermicelli is available in packets from most supermarkets.

PREPARATION TIME: *25 minutes*
COOKING TIME: *10 minutes*
SERVES 4–6

1 × 100 g packet Chinese vermicelli
oil, for deep-frying
1 teaspoon oil
2 teaspoons grated fresh ginger
1 tablespoon finely chopped coriander

1 clove garlic, finely diced
1 onion, cut into thin wedges
1 red capsicum, cut into strips
1 green capsicum, cut into strips
1 large carrot, cut into thin strips
400 g can baby corn, drained
400 g can straw mushrooms, drained
½ cup soy sauce
¼ cup malt vinegar
2 teaspoons brown sugar
1 teaspoon preserved chopped chilli
½ cup coriander leaves, for garnish

1 Deep-fry Chinese vermicelli in hot oil. Drain on absorbent paper. Place on a large serving plate and keep warm.
2 Heat teaspoon of oil in a large pan. Add ginger, coriander and garlic and cook for 2 minutes. Add onion, red and green capsicum and carrot. Stir-fry for 3 minutes. Add corn, mushrooms, combined soy, vinegar, brown sugar and chilli. Stir to combine and cook over a high heat for 3 minutes.
3 Spoon vegetables over noodles, pour over any remaining sauce. Garnish with coriander leaves, and serve.

Pasta with Spicy Pea Sauce

Dried yellow split peas have been used as the base for this sauce. They do not require soaking. Fresh fettuccine has been used in this recipe, but dried may be successfully substituted.

PREPARATION TIME: *30 minutes*
COOKING TIME: *10 minutes*
SERVES: 4–6

2 cups yellow split peas
1 tablespoon olive oil
1 onion chopped
1 clove garlic, crushed
¼ teaspoon chilli powder
½ teaspoon tumeric
½ teaspoon ground coriander
1 teaspoon ground allspice
¼ cup lemon juice
2 teaspoons grated lemon rind
500 g fresh fettuccine
fresh coriander sprigs, for garnish

1 Place peas in a large pan. Cover with cold water. Bring to the boil and boil, uncovered, for 25 minutes. Drain.
2 Heat oil in a pan. Add onion and garlic and cook over a low heat for 2 minutes. Add spices, stirring for 2 minutes. Add well-drained peas, lemon juice and rind. Stir to combine and cook over a low heat for 8–10 minutes.
3 Cook pasta in large quantity boiling water until just tender. Drain and place on a large serving plate. Pour sauce over pasta and garnish with coriander. Serve immediately.

Citrus Risotto

Rice cooked in the rind and juice of lemons and oranges makes an interesting and refreshing accompaniment to any meal. Shredded rind is long pieces of thinly cut rind, free of any pith.

PREPARATION TIME: *20 minutes*
COOKING TIME: *30 minutes*
SERVES 4–6

Excess orange and lemon rinds can be peeled thinly and cut into fine strips, blanched in boiling water, drained, then stored in a thick, clear, sugar syrup. Use the citrus-flavoured syrup to brush over cakes, and the rind to decorate cakes and salads.

1 tablespoon olive oil
2 cloves garlic, crushed
1 onion, finely chopped
1¼ cups short grain rice
2 teaspoons grated lemon rind
2 teaspoons grated orange rind
¼ cup lemon juice
½ cup orange juice
3½ cups hot vegetable stock or water
1 tablespoon shredded orange rind, for garnish
1 tablespoon shredded lemon rind, for garnish

1 Heat oil in a large pan. Add garlic and onion and cook over a low heat for 2–3 minutes. Stir in rice, making sure grains are well-coated in oil. Add grated lemon and orange rind, juices and stock or water. Bring to the boil, then reduce heat to a simmer. Cover and cook for 25 minutes or until rice is tender.
2 Place rice on a serving plate, garnished with combined shredded orange and lemon rind. Serve.

How many times does a recipe call for a squeeze of lemon juice which is usually about a tablespoon worth — and you only have a large lemon that you don't want to cut and then leave spoiling in the refrigerator? Simply pierce the lemon with a sharp skewer and squeeze out the desired amount of juice. Wrap the lemon in plastic wrap and refrigerate it until you next require a squeeze of lemon juice. An average lemon will yield about 3 tablespoons of juice.

Mozzarella and Zucchini Macaroni

Mozzarella and Zucchini Macaroni

Piping hot macaroni and zucchini coated with mozzarella and eggs produces a rich dish. Do not allow zucchini to overcook or brown.

PREPARATION TIME: *15 minutes*
COOKING TIME: *5 minutes*
SERVES 4–6

500 g spiral pasta
1 tablespoon olive oil
2 cloves garlic, cut into thin slivers
500 g small zucchini, sliced into rounds
250 g grated mozzarella
2 eggs, lightly beaten
freshly ground black pepper

1 Cook pasta in a large quantity of boiling water until just tender.
2 Heat oil in a large pan. Add garlic and cook for 2–3 minutes. Add zucchini and cook over a medium heat until tender. Do not allow zucchini to colour.
3 Drain pasta and place in a large bowl. Add mozzarella, eggs and black pepper. Stir to completely combine. Add zucchini and mix gently. Serve immediately.

Spaghetti with Walnut Sauce

A rich, spicy Italian-inspired sauce. The sauce is served with wholemeal spaghetti, topped with crispy fried wholemeal croûtons flavoured with cinnamon. The seeds are removed from tomatoes as they can impart a bitterness to the sauce.

PREPARATION TIME: *30 minutes*
COOKING TIME: *15 minutes*
SERVES 6

500 g dried wholemeal spaghetti
1 teaspoon olive oil
125 g walnuts, roughly chopped
1 onion, chopped
1 clove garlic, crushed
1 teaspoon ground cinnamon
1 teaspoon ground allspice
250 g button mushrooms, sliced
6 tomatoes, skin and seeds removed and chopped
1 tablespoon tomato paste
1 teaspoon lemon juice
1 teaspoon brown sugar
extra 1 tablespoon olive oil
2 slices wholegrain bread cut into 1 cm squares
extra 1 teaspoon ground cinnamon

1 Cook pasta in a large quantity of boiling water until just tender.
2 While pasta is cooking heat oil in a pan. Add walnuts and cook for 3–4 minutes until lightly browned. Remove and set aside.
3 Add onion, garlic and spices to pan. Cook for 3–4 minutes. Add mushrooms and cover and cook over a gentle heat for 5 minutes. Add tomatoes, tomato paste, lemon juice and brown sugar. Simmer, uncovered, for 10 minutes.
4 Heat extra oil in another pan. Stir in cinnamon, then add bread squares and cook until golden brown. Stir walnuts into sauce.
5 Combine spaghetti and sauce. Serve on a large platter, sprinkled with croûtons.
Note: For variety use a different shaped or coloured fresh or dried pasta. If using fresh pasta a short cooking time of only 2–3 minutes is required.

Above: Spaghetti with Walnut Sauce. Below: Citrus Risotto (page 47)

Shoya, tamari and soya are all soya sauces which are used for flavourings in savoury food. Shoya and tamari are favoured by the health conscious because they are naturally fermented from soya beans with barley or wheat, with no additives, whereas soya sauce may have the addition of sugar and salt. When a recipe calls for soy or soya sauce, any can be used giving slight flavour differences.

Brown Rice and Lentil Pilaf

This high fibre combination of rice and lentils is suitable as a main course dish.

PREPARATION TIME: *15 minutes*
COOKING TIME: *45 minutes*
SERVES 4–6

1 tablespoon olive oil
1 clove garlic, crushed
1 onion chopped
2 stalks celery, chopped
1 cup brown rice
¾ cup brown lentils
2 cups tomato juice
2 cups water
2 tablespoons soy sauce
2 zucchini, sliced
2 small thin eggplants, sliced
2 tablespoons toasted sesame seeds

1 Heat oil in a large pan. Add garlic, onion and celery and cook over a gentle heat for 3–4 minutes. Add rice and lentils and cook, stirring, for 4 minutes.
2 Combine tomato juice, water and soy sauce and pour over vegetables in pan. Cover tightly and cook over a gentle heat for 30–40 minutes or until both rice and lentils are tender. Add zucchini and eggplants and stir to combine. Cover and cook a further 3 minutes.
3 Spoon pilaf onto a large serving platter. Sprinkle over sesame seeds and serve.

Chick peas, also known as garbanzos, are a staple food in the Middle East. The peas are used whole, ground into flour or even cooked and mashed into a paste. Canned chick peas are available in delicatessens and specialty ingredient shops. Dried peas are best soaked overnight before cooking.

Coconut Rice

Basmati rice is a long grain rice used extensively in India. The rice has a mild aromatic flavour that teams well with spices, dried fruits and nuts. Basmati rice is available from most supermarkets. You can use the slightly less expensive jasmine rice if basmati is unavailable.

PREPARATION TIME: *5 minutes*
COOKING TIME: *15 minutes*
SERVES 4–6

1 teaspoon vegetable oil
1 teaspoon ground cardamom
1 cup shredded coconut
2 cups basmati rice
½ cup pistachio nuts
½ cup raisins

1 Heat oil in a large, heavy-based pan. Add cardamom and shredded coconut. Cook 2–3 minutes, stirring continuously, until coconut is pale golden brown.
2 Add rice and stir to combine. Pour on enough cold water to come 1 cm above the level of the rice. Bring rice to the boil and allow to boil until tunnels form in the rice. Reduce heat to very low, cover tightly and cook for 12 minutes, or until rice is tender.
3 Stir through nuts and raisins to combine. Replace lid and cook a further 3 minutes. Serve with a vegetable curry.

Chick Peas with Yoghurt

Dried chick peas do require long soaking and cooking but are well worth the time. Chick peas can also be bought in cans. Sold as 'Garbonzo' beans, you will find them at most health food stores. They require no soaking.

PREPARATION TIME: *1 hour*
COOKING TIME: *2 hours*
SERVES 4–6

1 cup dried chick peas
1 small whole peeled onion
1 small whole peeled garlic clove
2 bay leaves
1 tablespoon vegetable oil
1 teaspoon garam masala
1 teaspoon ground coriander
1 cup plain yoghurt
½ cup roughly chopped mint

1 Place chick peas in a large pan. Cover with cold water and bring to the boil. Boil for 2–3 minutes, then turn off heat. Cover and leave to stand for 1 hour. The peas should double in bulk. Drain, then cover with fresh cold water. Add onion, garlic

and bay leaves. Bring to the boil, cover and cook until beans are tender (about 2 hours).

2 Heat oil in a large pan. Stir in garam masala and ground coriander. Cook over a low heat for 2–3 minutes. Add chick peas and cook over a gentle heat until chick peas have golden brown spots.

3 Place chick peas in a large serving bowl. Spoon over yoghurt and top with mint. Serve with steamed fragrant rice and spicy mango chutney.

Clockwise from top: Coconut Rice, Chick Peas with Yoghurt and Brown Rice Lentil Pilaf

Wheat Pilaf

Whole wheat kernels are available from most health food stores. Whole wheat has a delicious nutty flavour with a slightly chewy texture. It can be served wherever a rice pilaf is normally served.

PREPARATION TIME: *20 minutes*
COOKING TIME: *1 hour*
SERVES 4–6

1 tablespoon vegetable oil
2 onions, finely chopped
1 cup finely chopped celery
1 large carrot, coarsely grated
1½ cups whole wheat
3 cups vegetable stock
1 tablespoon butter
¼ cup finely chopped parsley, for garnish

1 Heat oil in a large, heavy-based pan. Add onion and cook over a low heat until golden brown. Add celery, carrot and whole wheat. Stir to combine.
2 Pour in vegetable stock and bring to the boil. Reduce to a simmer, cover and cook over a low heat for 50–60 minutes or until wheat is soft. Stir butter into pilaf just prior to serving. Garnish with parsley and serve.

Wheat Pilaf

Warm Rice and Date Salad

This tropically inspired salad combines warm rice, dates and banana with a brown sugar dressing and is topped with macadamia nuts. Served with salad greens, this dish makes an interesting start to any meal.

PREPARATION TIME: *25 minutes*
COOKING TIME: *Nil*
SERVES 4–6

½ cup wild rice
¾ cup basmati or jasmine rice
1 cup chopped fresh dates
1 banana sliced
DRESSING
¼ cup olive oil
¼ cup lemon juice
2 teaspoons brown sugar
1 teaspoon French seeded mustard
⅓ cup toasted chopped macadamia nuts

1 Wash and drain wild rice. Add it to 450 mL boiling water. Cover and simmer for 45 minutes or until tender.
2 Wash basmati rice well. Place in a pan with cold water to cover 1 cm above the level of the rice. Bring to the boil, then cover tightly and cook for 10–15 minutes, or until tender.
3 Combine oil, lemon juice, brown sugar and mustard in a screw-top jar. Shake well to combine.
4 Combine rice, dates and banana. Pour over dressing and stir gently to combine. Place on a serving plate and garnish with macadamia nuts. Serve immediately.

Pasta with Lentils and Spinach

Red lentils do not require soaking. Pasta of any shape may be used for this recipe. Pine nuts can be toasted by placing on an overproof dish. Bake in moderate oven until golden brown.

PREPARATION TIME: *20 minutes*
COOKING TIME: *10 minutes*
SERVES 4–6

1 cup red lentils
500 g dried wholemeal spaghetti
15 g butter
1 teaspoon ground nutmeg
1 onion, finely chopped
6 spinach leaves, washed and shredded
1 tablespoon lemon juice
¼ cup toasted pine nuts

1 Cook lentils in boiling water until tender. Cook pasta in a large quantity of boiling water until just tender.
2 Whilst lentils and pasta are cooking, melt butter in a pan. Add nutmeg and onion and cook over a gentle heat until onion is soft. Add spinach, cover and cook until spinach is just tender.
3 Drain lentils. Add lemon juice; stirring to combine. Drain pasta. Combine lentils, pasta and spinach. Place on a serving plate, and sprinkle with pine nuts. Serve immediately.

Pasta with Lentils and Spinach

Aubergines, or eggplants as they are more commonly known, are fast becoming one of the most popular vegetables. The name 'eggplant' refers to the shape. There are many variates of eggplant ranging from white and round to small, long and black, the most common being the large, egg-shaped, rich purple eggplant. When purchasing eggplants, choose medium-sized, firm, smooth, shiny vegetables, free from blemishes. Eggplants are usually salted for a time to remove their bitter flavour and excess moisture. The term for this is often referred to as 'degorging'. It is a simple process: the eggplant is sliced or chopped, sprinkled with salt and left to stand and drain in a colander for 30–60 minutes. The eggplant is then rinsed in cold water and dried well with absorbent paper, before cooking as directed.

Burghul Wheat Patties with Ginger Mint Sauce

Burghul wheat and brown rice form the base of this easy-to-make patty that has a wonderful nutty flavour. Small dollops of the mixture are spooned into a small amount of oil and fried until golden brown. Ginger and mint combined make a fresh tangy sauce to accompany the patties.

PREPARATION TIME: *15 minutes +*
2 hours soaking
COOKING TIME: *10 minutes*
SERVES 4–6

1 cup burghul wheat, covered and soaked in cold water for 2 hours
1½ cups cooked brown rice
1 onion, finely chopped
¼ cup chopped mint
2 eggs lightly beaten
¼ cup wholemeal flour
oil, for shallow frying
SAUCE
1 teaspoon olive oil
1 tablespoon finely grated ginger
1 teaspoon raw sugar
½ cup white wine vinegar
¼ cup water
½ cup chopped mint

1 Drain burghul wheat, and remove excess moisture by squeezing it with your hands. Combine burghul, brown rice, onion, mint, eggs and flour. Mix well to combine.
2 Prepare the sauce by heating the oil in pan. Add grated ginger and cook over a gentle heat for 2–3 minutes. Add sugar, vinegar and water. Simmer, stirring, 2–3 minutes. Cool to lukewarm, then stir in mint.
3 Heat oil in large pan. Place spoonfuls of mixture into moderately hot oil and cook until golden brown on both sides. Drain on absorbent paper. Keep warm until all patties are made.
4 Serve patties with ginger and mint sauce.

Baked Eggplant and Rice

This is a recipe that is sure to tantalise the taste buds: eggplant baked with onions, capsicums, lemon and capers, covered with a flavoursome sauce.

PREPARATION TIME: *30 minutes*
COOKING TIME: *25 minutes*
SERVES 4–6

1 large eggplant
1 tablespoon olive oil
2 Spanish onions, sliced
1 red capsicum, sliced
1 green capsicum, sliced
2 lemons, sliced
2 tablespoons capers
½ cup red wine vinegar
2 tablespoons brown sugar
¼ cup sultanas
RICE
1 teaspoon olive oil
1 teaspoon turmeric
1 cup long grain rice
2 teaspoons finely grated lemon rind
2 cups vegetable stock

1 Cut eggplant into 1 cm thick slices. Place in colander, sprinkle with salt and leave to stand 30 minutes. Rinse eggplant under cold water, drain and dry using absorbent paper.
2 Brush a shallow ovenproof dish with oil. Place eggplant slices in the dish, in a single layer, and brush with oil. Top with onion, capsicum and lemon slices. Sprinkle over capers.
3 Combine vinegar, brown sugar and sultanas. Pour over eggplant mixture. Cover and bake at 180°C for 25 minutes.
4 Prepare rice whilst eggplant is baking. Heat oil in a heavy-based pan. Add turmeric and rice and stir until rice grains are well-coated with oil. Add lemon rind and stock. Bring to the boil, and boil until all water has evaporated and tunnels have formed. Reduce to a very low heat, cover and cook for 12 to 15 minutes or until rice is tender.
5 Serve rice on a large platter or individual plates, topped with the eggplant mixture.

Above: Burghul Wheat Patties with Ginger Mint Sauce. Below: Baked Eggplant and Rice

SPECIAL FLAVOUR ADDITIONS

Having the right ingredients on hand enables the vegetarian cook to produce quick and easy meals with the minimum of effort and with maximum effect. No store cupboard is complete without a few 'essential' ingredients that offer instant inspiration, these basics can transform a simple plate of steamed vegetables, pasta or rice into an innovative meal.

Take stock of your store cupboard, by now you should have a good range of staple ingredients like grains, cereals, beans, spices and flavourings. To this base, add the following indispensable extras — jars of black and green olives, capers, canned plum tomatoes, bottled vegetables such as artichokes and marinated mushrooms, dried tomatoes, good quality olive oil and a small selection of vinegars, mustard, mayonnaise and Indian-style bottled chutneys and relishes. Keep a wedge of fresh Parmesan cheese, feta cheese, yoghurt and unsalted butter on hand in the refrigerator. A supply of fresh herbs is also vital as are lemons, garlic, and chillies. The freezer should hold supplies of wholemeal bread sticks, foccacia, pizza bases and flat breads (many of the breads in our breads and baking section can be successfully frozen), ready-rolled puff and short crust pastry and the essential filo pastry.

Other essentials that are the foundation to many dishes include the popular pesto sauce, traditionally made with basil, pine nuts and fresh Parmesan, we now see it made with other fresh herbs like coriander or flat-leaved parsley (see our recipe for Pasta with Coriander Pesto page 42). Pesto is ideal to serve with hot pasta, steamed vegetables and spread on pizza bases and topped with fresh tomato. Place pesto in a small jar, cover with a 2 cm layer of oil and store in the refrigerator for up to two weeks. Olive Paste (see our recipe page 8) is perfect to serve with fresh bread, crisp vegetables and hard boiled eggs for an easy alfresco meal. Use it to top foccacia, add a spoonful to omelette fillings, stir a teaspoon into a basic oil and vinegar dressing. Remember with the right ingredients on hand you have the ability to create simple yet delicious vegetarian meals instantly. Use all of these store cupboard essentials to build up your culinary repertoire.

Here are three of the most useful 'essential ingredients':

Walnut and Garlic Sauce

This rich sauce is the perfect dressing for hot pasta, steamed seasonal vegetables, particularly beans, potatoes and broccoli. It makes a wonderful flavouring for soup, just add a spoonful at serving time.
Makes 1 cup

100 g walnut halves
4 cloves garlic, peeled
2 cups olive oil
¼ cup white wine vinegar
salt

1 Place walnuts on a baking tray, cook in a moderate oven 180°C for about 5 minutes. Cool.
2 Peel garlic cloves, place walnuts and garlic in a food processor, process until finely ground. Add oil in a slow stream, with food processor operating, until thick and creamy. Slowly add vinegar and salt to taste.
3 Place in a small clean jar, cover with a thin layer of oil, store in the refrigerator for up to one week. Pour away oil before using.

Place garlic cloves and walnuts in processor, process until ground.

Add oil in a thin stream, with food processor operating, until creamy.

Seasonal Pesto

In this recipe we have used basil and parsley, if basil is in season use all basil. Pine nuts can be replaced by walnuts.
Makes 2 cups

4 cloves garlic, peeled
2 cups fresh basil leaves
1 cup parsley sprigs
⅔ cup pine nuts
1½ cups grated Parmesan cheese
1½ cups olive oil

1 Place garlic, basil, parsley, pine nuts and Parmesan cheese in a food processor or blender. Blend at medium speed, adding oil in a thin stream until smooth.
2 Place in a clean jar, cover with a thin layer of oil, store in the refrigerator for up to two weeks. Pour away oil before using.

Place garlic, basil and parsley in the processor with Parmesan cheese.

Place pesto in clean jar, cover with a thin layer of oil. Refrigerate.

Roasted Garlic Paste

Yes, it is correct we have called for 10 bulbs of garlic in this recipe. The result will be a morish, sweet, roasted garlic paste that blends delightfully with pasta and rice dishes, vegetables and breads.
Makes 1 cup.

10 bulbs garlic
2 tablespoons olive oil
⅓ cup water

1 Remove the loose papery skin from garlic bulbs. Place garlic in a greased baking dish, pour over oil and water.
2 Cook garlic in a moderate oven 180°C for about 1 hour or until garlic is very soft. Spoon oil and water from baking dish over garlic as they cook, add a little more water to baking dish if it drys out. Remove garlic from oven and cool.
3 Separate the garlic cloves, press the cooked garlic out of their skins into a small bowl. Mash garlic with a fork until smooth.
4 Store in an airtight container for up to three days.

Place garlic bulbs in baking dish, pour over water and oil, bake.

Separate the garlic cloves. Press the cooked garlic out of their skins.

Pies, Pancakes, Tarts and More

THIS CHAPTER IS bursting with hearty main course dishes. It includes rich, golden pies and tarts, flavour filled vegetable pancakes and patties, spicy casseroles, curries and more. By combining the freshest seasonal vegetables with wholefoods we have produced the very best of vegetarian cuisine from countries the world over. The emphasis is on good health and great tasting recipes.

There is robust winter fare that includes Vegetable Goulash and Dumplings, Mushroom Strudel, Vegetable and Coconut Curry and light and easy warmer weather dishes like Apple and Camembert Tart, Peanut Patties with Garlic Mayonnaise and Satay Vegetable and Sprout Pancakes.

Above: Satay Vegetable and Sprout Pancakes (page 60). Below: Potato and Onion Tart (page 60)

Potato and Onion Tart

This golden Potato and Onion Tart can be accompanied by salad or vegetables of your choice. The pastry case can be prepared and baked the day before required.

PREPARATION TIME: *30 minutes +*
1 hour chilling
COOKING TIME: *25 minutes*
SERVES: *4–6*

PASTRY
185 g butter
1 tablespoon iced water
1 tablespoon lemon juice
2 cups wholemeal plain flour
FILLING
1 tablespoon olive oil
4 large brown onions, thinly sliced
2 large ripe tomatoes, peeled and chopped
1 teaspoon brown sugar
1 teaspoon malt vinegar
extra 1 tablespoon olive oil
6 medium potatoes, peeled, thinly sliced
1 cup sour cream
½ teaspoon paprika

1 To make Pastry: Place butter, iced water and lemon juice into a large bowl. Add quarter cup of the flour and mix to form a paste using a fork. Add remaining flour and mix to form a smooth dough. Wrap in plastic wrap and refrigerate for 1 hour.
2 To prepare Filling: Heat oil in a large pan. Add onions and cook, stirring over a low heat until they are a golden brown. Add tomatoes, sugar and vinegar. Stir to combine. Simmer, uncovered, until thickened.
3 Heat extra oil in a large, shallow pan. Add potatoes in a single layer. Cook, turning once, until potatoes are golden brown.
4 Roll out pastry between two sheets of greaseproof paper to fit a 23 cm fluted flan tin. Line tin with pastry and bake blind for 25–30 minutes or until crisp and golden brown.
5 Spread onion filling over the base of the cooked pastry. Arrange the potatoes on top of the onion filling. Spread over sour cream and sprinkle with paprika. Bake in a hot oven, 200°C, for 8 minutes or until top is golden brown. Serve hot or at room temperature.

Satay Vegetable and Sprout Pancakes

Wholemeal pancakes filled with crunchy vegetables and sprouts, and topped with satay dressing make an appetising summer meal. The pancakes can be prepared the day before required and refrigerated until needed. Reheat in a low oven, covered with aluminium foil to prevent them drying out.

PREPARATION TIME: *35 minutes*
COOKING TIME: *15 minutes*
SERVES 4–6

PANCAKES
1¼ cups plain wholemeal flour
1 teaspoon baking powder
1 egg
1½ cups milk
1 teaspoon oil
FILLING
250 g fresh snow pea sprouts
250 g mung bean sprouts
6 spring onions, finely sliced
250 g button mushrooms, thinly sliced
1 large carrot, coarsely grated
1 cup roasted peanuts
extra ½ cup roasted peanuts, for garnish
DRESSING
½ cup crunchy peanut butter
2 tablespoons cider vinegar
2 tablespoons lemon juice
2 teaspoons sambal oelek

1 To prepare Pancakes: Sift flour and baking powder into a large bowl. Make a well in the centre. Combine egg, milk and oil and stir into flour. Mix until mixture forms a smooth batter. Pour batter into a jug.
2 Brush a heated pancake pan with oil. Pour in enough batter to thinly cover the base of the pan. Cook for 2–3 minutes until the mixture sets. Turn over using a

One of the first requirements for good cooking is a pepper mill, filled with whole black peppercorns that produces fresh, spicy pepper. Pepper is the fruit of the vine *Piper nigrum*. The tree produces long clusters of tiny berries. Black pepper is the fully ripened berries; white pepper is the inner part of the berry, exposed after the outer cover has been removed. White pepper can also be ground fresh, especially for use in white-based sauces and soups.

metal spatula, and cook a further 1–2 minutes. Remove, place onto plate and cover with square of greaseproof paper. Continue in this manner until all mixture has been used. Keep pancakes warm.

3 To make Filling: Combine prepared vegetables. Divide evenly between pancakes. Garnish pancakes with extra roasted nuts. Fold over each or roll up and place on a large platter or individual serving plates.

4 To make Dressing: Combine all ingredients in a small bowl, whisking well. Pour over pancakes or serve separately.

Vegetable Goulash and Dumplings

This goulash is flavoured with tomato and paprika and topped with crisp, caraway seed dumplings. If you prefer soft dumplings, simply cover the pan after the dumpling mixture has been added.

PREPARATION TIME: *30 minutes*
COOKING TIME: *65 minutes*
SERVES 4–6

30 g butter
1 clove garlic, crushed
2 onions, chopped
1 tablespoon sweet paprika
2 tablespoons plain flour
2 cups vegetable stock
2 tablespoons tomato paste
8 small new potatoes
8 whole baby carrots
1 turnip, peeled and cut into large dice
3 zucchini, cut into large pieces
425 g can whole tomatoes
1 tablespoon fresh thyme
1 cup light sour cream
DUMPLINGS
1 cup plain flour
1 teaspoon baking powder
1 teaspoon caraway seeds
30 g butter
⅓ cup milk

1 Melt the butter in a large pan. Add garlic and onions and cook over a low heat until onions are soft. Remove from heat.

Stir in paprika and flour. Gradually add vegetable stock. Return to heat and stir constantly until mixture boils and thickens. Stir in tomato paste.

2 Add vegetables, undrained canned tomatoes and thyme. Transfer mixture to a well-greased ovenproof dish. Cover and bake at 180°C for 40 minutes.

3 To prepare Dumplings: Sift flour and baking powder into a large bowl. Stir in caraway seeds, then rub in butter. Make a well in the centre and stir in the milk, using a table knife to form a soft dough.

4 Remove goulash from the oven and top with spoonfuls of dumpling mixture. Return to oven, uncovered, and cook for 20 minutes or until the dumplings are cooked and golden brown.

5 Serve with sour light cream.

Vegetable Goulash and Dumplings

Spanish Onion Torte

This Italian-inspired onion and potato torte is rich in colour and flavour. Serve with a spoonful of yoghurt and a crisp green salad.

PREPARATION TIME: *30 minutes*
COOKING TIME: *40 minutes*
SERVES 4–6

❦

Garlic is the most pungent of the onion family. It can be used whole, chopped or crushed. If a milder garlic flavour is desired, use a whole, peeled garlic and remove it before serving. Garlic odour can be removed from your hands by rubbing them with salt, bi-carbonate of soda or half a cut lemon.

1 teaspoon olive oil
2 large Spanish onions, thinly sliced
½ cup water
½ cup red wine
½ teaspoon dried rosemary
500 g potatoes, grated
⅓ cup natural yoghurt
1 tablespoon plain flour
1 egg
½ cup grated Parmesan cheese
¼ cup chopped Italian parsley

1 Heat oil in a heavy-based pan. Add onions, cook over a medium heat until tender. Add water and wine and simmer, uncovered, for about 20 minutes or until the liquid has evaporated and the onions are a dark reddish brown.
2 Combine rosemary, potatoes, yoghurt, flour, egg and Parmesan cheese. Add onions.
3 Spread the mixture evenly into a well-greased 25 cm ovenproof flan dish. Bake at 200°C, for 35–40 minutes until golden brown. Sprinkle with parsley, then cut into wedges and serve.

Spanish Onion Torte

Sweet Potato and Chilli Flan

An unusual but wonderfully colourful combination of ingredients that reflect a strong Mexican influence make up this hot and spicy pie. The crust (croustade) can be prepared and baked the day before required.

PREPARATION TIME: *40 minutes*
COOKING TIME: *15 minutes*
SERVES 4–6

❦

CRUST
1½ cups wholemeal breadcrumbs
½ cup wholemeal plain flour
½ cup oatbran
125 g butter, melted
FILLING
300 g orange sweet potato
2 tablespoons orange juice
2 teaspoons finely grated orange rind
1 teaspoon vegetable oil
1 fresh red chilli, finely chopped
1 cup cooked red kidney beans
1 large ripe avocado, diced
1 cup grated Cheddar cheese

1 To make the Crust: Combine breadcrumbs, flour and oatbran in a bowl. Make a well in the centre and add melted butter. Mix well. Press mixture into well-greased 20 cm pie plate. Bake at 180°C for 20–25 minutes.
2 To make Filling: Cook sweet potato in boiling water until tender. Drain and add orange juice and rind. Mash together well. Set aside.
3 Heat oil in a pan. Add chilli and cook over a gentle heat for 2 minutes. Add well drained kidney beans and cook for 2 minutes. Add avocado, stirring gently to combine.
4 Spread sweet potato mixture over the base of the crust. Top with the bean and avocado mixture. Sprinkle over cheese. Bake at 180°C for about 15 minutes or until golden brown. Serve in wedges accompanied by Spicy Salsa (see page 78) or chilli sauce.
Note: After preparing fresh chillies wash the chopping board, knife and hands thoroughly.

Above: Sweet Potato and Chilli Flan. Below: Eggplant and Sun-dried Tomato (page 64)

What is there to do with leftover bread but make breadcrumbs? Any bread can be used for crumbs but it is best if it is 2–3 days old. The crusts can also be used unless fresh, white breadcrumbs are required, in which case they should be removed. Bread crumbs can be made using a blender or food processor, or by pushing dried bread through a fine sieve.

Store them in something you can seal, then label and date them and freeze for future use. They can be used straight from the freezer.

Eggplant and Sun-dried Tomato

Large purple eggplant or aubergines as they are also known are a very versatile vegetable and this recipe is a perfect example. Serve with homemade sauces, relishes or salsa (see pages 78–79).

PREPARATION TIME: *30 minutes*
COOKING TIME: *10 minutes*
SERVES 6

2 large eggplants
salt
2 tablespoons olive oil
½ cup sun-dried tomatoes, chopped
¼ cup chopped pimento stuffed olives
¼ cup chopped pistachio nuts
¼ cup finely shredded basil
⅔ cup grated Pecorino or Parmesan cheese

1 Slice each eggplant into three thick slices. Sprinkle with salt, allow to stand for 30 minutes. Rinse well with cold water, drain and pat dry with absorbent paper.
2 Heat olive oil in shallow pan, cook eggplant on both sides until lightly golden. Place eggplant slices on a baking tray.
3 Combine sun-dried tomatoes, olives, pistachio nuts, basil and cheese. Spoon mixture evenly over eggplant slices and bake in a moderate oven 180°C for 10 minutes or until hot and bubbly. Serve with salad greens.
Note: Sun-dried tomatoes are preserved in olive oil. They are available in some supermarkets and good delicatessens.

Mushroom Strudel

The filling mixture must be cooled before placing it on filo pastry, to prevent the pastry from becoming soggy.

PREPARATION TIME: *20 minutes*
COOKING TIME: *25 minutes*
SERVES 4–6

15 g butter
1 clove garlic, crushed
2 teaspoons lemon juice
500 g medium mushroom caps, sliced
2 teaspoons finely grated lemon rind
freshly ground pepper
8 sheets filo pastry
3 tablespoons olive oil
½ cup grated pecorino cheese
6 spring onions, sliced
2 teaspoons poppy seeds

1 Melt butter in a medium-sized pan. Add garlic and lemon juice and cook over a low heat for 2 minutes. Add mushrooms, lemon rind and pepper. Cook until mushrooms are just tender.
2 Place filo on a large, flat surface, brushing every second sheet with oil. Place cooled filling along the centre, parallel with the long sides of the pastry. Top with cheese and spring onions. Roll up pastry, tucking in the ends. Place on a well-oiled tray, with the seam underneath. Brush top and sides with oil and sprinkle with poppy seeds.
3 Bake at 200°C for 8 minutes. Reduce heat to 180°C and cook for a further 15 minutes. Serve immediately with fresh seasonal salad greens.
Note: Place a slightly damp tea-towel over filo pastry while it is not being used.

Soya Bean Patties with Tahini Sauce

These well-flavoured soy beans are coated with sesame seeds and cooked until lightly golden. They are delicious served with Spicy Salsa (see page 78). Canned beans will save preparation time but, of course, fresh cooked beans could be used.

PREPARATION TIME: *25 minutes*
COOKING TIME: *20 minutes*
SERVES 6

1½ cups cooked soya beans
1 onion, finely chopped
1 tablespoon tomato paste
2 teaspoons chilli sauce
2 tablespoons finely chopped parsley

1 cup fresh wholemeal breadcrumbs
1 egg
¾ cup milk
1 cup packaged dry breadcrumbs
3 tablespoons sesame seeds
1 cup plain wholemeal flour
oil, for shallow frying
SAUCE
2 cloves garlic, crushed
½ cup tahini
¼ cup water
½ cup lemon juice

1 Mash beans using a potato masher. Add onion, tomato paste, chilli sauce, parsley and fresh breadcrumbs. Mix well to combine. Divide mixture into twelve even proportions. Shape into rounds and flatten with your fingers to form pattie shapes.

2 Combine egg and milk in one bowl, and breadcrumbs and sesame seeds in another bowl. Roll patties in flour, then dip each into combined egg and milk and coat with combined dry breadcrumbs and sesame seeds.

3 Heat oil in a large shallow pan. Cook patties on medium heat until golden brown on both sides. Drain on absorbent paper. Set aside and keep warm.

4 To prepare Sauce: Combine all ingredients in small bowl. Serve patties hot accompanied by tahini sauce.

Above: Soya Bean Patties. Below: Mushroom Strudel

Skim and low-fat milks are becoming commonplace in our diets as we realise the need to reduce fats and total kilojoules, but not the excellent source of calcium and minerals that they provide. All low-fat dairy foods can be used in place of their full-cream counterparts with little or no difference in cooking technique, flavour and appearance of the final product. There are a full selection of low-fat milks on the market to suit your tastes and/or dietary needs.

Peanut Patties with Garlic Mayonnaise

You can use roasted or raw, salted or unsalted peanuts for this dish.

PREPARATION TIME: *20 minutes*
COOKING TIME: *15 minutes*
SERVES 4–6

1 cup finely chopped peanuts
½ cup brown rice flour
½ cup rice bran
1 onion, finely chopped
1 teaspoon ground coriander
1 teaspoon ground cumin
¼ teaspoon ground chilli powder
¾ cup soya milk
oil, for shallow frying
GARLIC MAYONNAISE
1 cup mayonnaise
2 cloves garlic, crushed
2 tablespoons finely chopped chives
2 tablespoons finely chopped parsley
1 tablespoon white wine vinegar

1 Combine peanuts, brown rice flour, rice bran, onion and spices in a large bowl. Stir in soya milk to form a soft mixture.
2 Heat oil in a large, shallow pan. Place spoonfuls of mixture into hot oil. Cook on both sides until golden brown and cooked through. Drain on absorbent paper. Set aside and keep warm.
3 To prepare Mayonnaise: Combine all ingredients in a small basin. Mix well to combine. Serve with garlic mayonnaise.

Peanut Patties with Garlic Mayonnaise

Onion and Black Olive Pie

Light, crispy, puff pastry is filled with a colourful combination of food. The onion and olives are cooked in the red wine vinegar to form a relish-like mixture. The pie can be eaten hot or cold.

PREPARATION TIME: *25 minutes*
COOKING TIME: *35 minutes*
SERVES 6

1 × 375 g packet frozen puff pastry, thawed
1 teaspoon olive oil
2 onions, thinly sliced
¼ cup red wine vinegar
125 g black olives, stoned and roughly chopped
4 hard boiled eggs, roughly chopped
100 g feta cheese, crumbled
½ small red capsicum, chopped
1 egg, lightly beaten, for glazing

1 Roll out the pastry on a lightly floured surface. Cut into a 30 cm circle. Leave to rest while preparing filling.
2 Heat oil in a small, shallow pan. Add onions and cook gently until onions are golden brown. Add vinegar and olives and cook, uncovered, until mixture becomes thick and sticky. Allow to cool to room temperature.
3 Place pastry round onto a lightly greased, large flat baking tray. Spread onion and olive filling over one half of the pastry. Top with eggs, cheese and capsicum. Brush edge with egg, fold over unfilled side of pastry and press down gently to seal, 1 cm from pastry edge.
4 Glaze the top of pie with remaining egg. Make slits in the top. Bake at 200°C for 15 minutes. Reduce heat to 180°C and cook for 20 minutes or until pastry is golden brown. Serve hot or cold.
Note: When buying onions choose onions that are dry and firm with a smooth papery skin. To avoid tears while cutting onions leave root end on as a pungent odour is released when the root end is removed, making you cry. Red or Spanish onions may be used in this recipe to create a sweeter tasting pie.

Above: Onion and Black Olive Pie. Below: Pumpkin Croquettes with Watercress Sauce (page 68)

Pumpkin Croquettes with Watercress Sauce

Croquettes are traditionally a mixture of savoury foods bound together and shaped into a barrel or cigar shape and deep fried. This recipe is exactly that, using classic ingredients with updated flavour combinations.

PREPARATION TIME: *40 minutes*
COOKING TIME: *15 minutes*
SERVES 4–6

500 g pumpkin, cut into pieces
3 spring onions, finely chopped
1 teaspoon sesame seeds
1 egg, lightly beaten
1 cup wholemeal plain flour
2 eggs, lightly beaten
½ cup skim milk
1½ cups oatbran
oil, for deep-frying
SAUCE
½ bunch watercress washed, leaves removed from stalks
3 spring onions, finely chopped
2 tablespoons capers
1 cup natural yoghurt
freshly ground pepper

1 Place pumpkin in a large pan and cover it with cold water. Bring to the boil, reduce heat, then cover and simmer until pumpkin is tender. Drain and mash. Add spring onions, sesame seeds and egg. Beat with a wooden spoon until smooth.
2 Divide mixture into twelve equal portions. Roll into small balls or barrel shapes. Coat with flour, combined eggs and milk, then coat with oatbran.
3 Finely chop watercress leaves. Combine watercress, spring onions, capers, yoghurt and freshly ground pepper to taste.
4 Deep-fry croquettes in moderately hot oil until golden brown and crisp. Drain on absorbent paper and keep warm.
5 Serve pumpkin croquettes with watercress sauce and seasonal green salad.

Vegetable Dumplings with Black Bean Sauce

Chinese steamed dumplings filled with a combination of vegetables and served with black bean sauce make an interesting main course meal. Dried black beans are available from Asian speciality stores. They must be rinsed to remove the excess salt that they have been preserved in.

PREPARATION TIME: *1 hour 15 minutes*
COOKING TIME: *30 minutes*
SERVES 4–6

DUMPLINGS
3 cups plain flour
1 tablespoon baking powder
60 g butter
¾ cup warm water
1 teaspoon white vinegar
12 squares greaseproof paper
2 teaspoons vegetable oil
1 teaspoon sesame oil
FILLING
1 teaspoon vegetable oil
2 spring onions, finely chopped
1 stick celery, finely chopped
6 medium-sized radishes, finely chopped
½ cup finely chopped bamboo shoots
⅓ cup chopped water chestnuts
2 tablespoons soy sauce
SAUCE
2 tablespoons dried black beans
¼ cup honey
½ cup brown vinegar
2 cloves garlic, crushed
1 teaspoon finely grated ginger
1 tablespoon cornflour
¾ cup water

1 Sift flour and baking powder into a large basin. Rub in butter until mixture resembles fine breadcrumbs. Make a well in the centre and stir in combined water and vinegar to form a soft pliable dough. Turn out onto a lightly floured surface and knead lightly. Cover and wrap with plastic wrap and stand for 30 minutes.
2 Prepare filling while pastry is resting. Heat oil in a medium-sized pan. Add prepared vegetables and cook, shaking the pan, for 3–4 minutes. Add soy sauce, cover and cook for 3 minutes. Remove from heat and allow to cool.

Re-knead rested dough and form into a long sausage shape, cut into 12 equal pieces.

Knead each of the 12 pieces into a ball; and then roll each ball into a 10 cm circle.

Place heaped teaspoonfuls of filling into centre of each, gather edges and twist to seal.

3 Re-knead rested dough and form into a long sausage shape, divide into twelve equal pieces. Knead each portion into a ball, and roll each ball into a 10 cm circle. Place a heaped teaspoonful of filling in the centre, gather in the edges and twist to seal.

4 Brush paper squares with combined vegetable and sesame oil. Place dumplings smooth side down on paper. Arrange dumplings in a single layer in the steamer and cook over simmering water for 30 minutes.

5 Prepare sauce whilst dumplings are cooking. Place beans in a sieve and rinse under cold running water for 3 minutes. Drain and chop. Combine beans, honey, vinegar, garlic and ginger in a small pan and cook for 3 minutes over a low heat. Blend cornflour with water and add to sauce. Stir continuously until mixture boils and thickens. Serve dumplings with black bean sauce.

Vegetable Dumplings with Black Bean Sauce

Clockwise from top: Vegetable and Coconut Curry (page 71), Combination Nut Curry (page 71) and Spiced Potato Pancakes (page 76)

Vegetable and Coconut Curry

This combination of vegetables is cooked in spices and coconut milk. It makes a perfect winter's fireside meal, served with fragrant rice and side dishes of cucumber with yoghurt and fiery pickles. Curry can be made up to a day before required.

PREPARATION TIME: *30 minutes*
COOKING TIME: *20 minutes*
SERVES 4–6

30 g butter
1 large onion, sliced
2 fresh green chillies, finely chopped
2 cloves garlic, crushed
2 teaspoons finely grated ginger
1 teaspoon turmeric
1 teaspoon ground cardamom
1 teaspoon ground cinnamon
2 cups coconut milk
2 strips lemon rind
125 g small fresh green beans, trimmed
1 green capsicum, cut into strips
1 red capsicum, cut into strips
½ small cauliflower, cut into florets
3 zucchini, cut into thick rounds
125 g small yellow squash, cut in halves
4 large potatoes, cut into large dice
½ cup coconut cream
½ cup fresh coriander leaves, chopped

1 In a large, heavy-based pan melt butter over a low heat. Add onion, chilli, garlic and ginger. Cook for 3–4 minutes until onions are soft. Add turmeric, cardamom and cinnamon and cook, stirring, for 2–3 minutes.
2 Add coconut milk and lemon rind. Simmer gently, uncovered, for 10 minutes. Add vegetables and cook, uncovered, until vegetables are just tender.
3 Add coconut cream and simmer for a further 5 minutes. Serve on a larger platter, garnished with coriander leaves.
Note: Coriander, sometimes called Chinese parsley has a unique flavour and lively scent, add the chopped leaves sparingly if you are not familiar with this zesty herb.

Any combination of fresh seasonal vegetables could be used for this creamy curry.

Combination Nut Curry

This is a traditional Indian-style curry that can be served as part of a curry meal or as a meal by itself, accompanied by fragrant Basmati rice — the traditional Indian rice.

PREPARATION TIME: *15 minutes*
COOKING TIME: *30 minutes*
SERVES 6

1 tablespoon vegetable oil
2 cloves garlic, crushed
1 tablespoon finely grated ginger
2 onions, finely chopped
1 small red chilli, finely chopped
1 teaspoon turmeric
1 teaspoon ground cardamom
2 teaspoons grated lime rind
1 tablespoon lime juice
3 cups coconut cream
250 g macadamia nuts
125 g raw peanuts
125 g almond kernels
1 bunch coriander, roughly chopped
½ cup toasted shredded coconut

1 Heat oil in a large pan. Add garlic, ginger, onions and chilli. Cook over a gentle heat until the onions are soft. Add turmeric, cardamom, lime rind and juice. Cook, stirring for 2 minutes.
2 Add coconut cream, stirring to combine. Bring to the boil, then reduce to a simmer. Add nuts and simmer uncovered for 8–10 minutes. Stir in coriander and simmer for another 5 minutes.
3 Place the mixture into a large serving bowl and sprinkle over coconut. Serve with rice, toasted papadums and spicy pickles and chutneys.

Nuts are one of the most versatile and useful foods available to us. They can be eaten at any time, as part of a meal or as a snack. Together with grains and green vegetables, they form a nutritionally balanced main course meal. Combined with dried fruits, they are a conveniently, healthy snack. Nuts have a high fat content and should be stored in a dry cool place. If stored in a sealed glass container their shelf-life, is up to 3 months. For longer storage, they can be frozen for up to 6 months. Nuts that have been chopped or ground should be eaten within 4–6 weeks.

Try grinding your own nuts at home if you have a mortar and pestle, food processor, blender, or an electric or handheld coffee grinder. You will find the freshly ground nuts to have more flavour and the end result is more economical. Freshly ground nuts keep well in the freezer, stored in an airtight container.

Tomatoes are a versatile and indispensable fruit (yes, a fruit, not a vegetable). They are delicious when eaten raw, but they can also be baked, puréed and stuffed. They are a basic ingredient of many sauces, soups and stews, and are frequently used to enhance a wide variety of dishes. Often a recipe will ask for the tomatoes to be peeled. This can be quite easily done by firstly cutting small crosses into the tops of firm ripe tomatoes, plunging them into boiling water for 2–3 minutes, then into iced water. Remove and peel. Some recipes will also ask for tomatoes to be deseeded — this is done because the seeds can impart a bitter flavour and also add too much water to the dish.

Individual Olive and Tomato Pies

These small pies are perfect as cold picnic fare, or served hot as a weekend meal for family or friends. Serve with homemade or purchased Italian tomato sauce. Try serving them with Fresh Tomato Relish (see page 79) or Spicy Salsa (see page 78).

PREPARATION TIME: *30 minutes +*
20 minutes chilling
COOKING TIME: *15 minutes*
SERVES 4–6

PASTRY
3 cups wholemeal self-raising flour
125 g butter
¾–1 cup iced water
milk, for glazing
FILLING
1 teaspoon olive oil
1 spring onion, chopped
2 firm tomatoes, peeled, deseeded and chopped
1½ cups finely chopped, stoned, black olives
¼ cup slivered almonds

1 To prepare Pastry: Sift flour into a large bowl and rub in butter. Make a well in the centre and add enough water to form a soft dough. Knead into a smooth round ball, wrap in plastic wrap and refrigerate for 20 minutes.
2 Prepare filling while the pastry is chilling. Heat oil in a small pan, add onion and cook over a gentle heat for 2 minutes. Add tomatoes and simmer, uncovered, until the sauce thickens. Stir in olives and almonds. Set aside and allow to cool.
3 Roll out pastry on a lightly floured board until it is 30 mm in thickness. Cut out rounds using a 5 cm cutter.
4 Place a teaspoonful of filling on half the rounds. Glaze edges with milk. Place remaining rounds on top and pinch edges together. Glaze the top of each pie with milk.
5 Bake at 220°C for 12–15 minutes or until golden brown.

Zucchini Tart

This is a great cook ahead meal for busy days, simply prepare potato base and filling the day before place in the greased pie plate, cover well and refrigerate. Before cooking simply combine the eggs, sour cream and milk, pour over filling and bake as directed.

PREPARATION TIME: *25 minutes*
COOKING TIME: *50 minutes*
SERVES 4–6

CRUST
4 large potatoes, peeled and cut into even-sized pieces
30 g butter
½ teaspoon ground nutmeg
FILLING
6 small zucchini, sliced
1 small onion, finely chopped
1 sprig fresh rosemary
2 tablespoons white wine
2 eggs
½ cup light sour cream
½ cup low-fat evaporated milk
2 tablespoons freshly grated Parmesan cheese

1 Boil or steam potatoes until soft. Drain and add butter and nutmeg. Mash, then beat with a wooden spoon until creamy.
2 Spoon potato into well-greased, 23 cm pie plate. Spread evenly over base and sides.
3 Place zucchini, onion, rosemary and wine in a small pan. Cover and cook over a low heat until just tender. Cool to room temperature. Place in the potato crust.
4 Beat together eggs, sour cream and milk. Pour over zucchini mixture, sprinkle with Parmesan. Bake in a moderate oven, 180°C, for 50 minutes. Serve warm.

Spinach Cheesecake

The process of lining the pastry with paper and weighting it down is known as 'blind' baking. By cooking the pastry this way, it will ensure a crisp dry pastry crust.

PREPARATION TIME: *30 minutes +*
20 minutes chilling
COOKING TIME: *40 minutes*
SERVES 4–6

CRUST
1¼ cups plain wholemeal flour
½ cup wheatgerm
125 g butter, chopped
1 tablespoon iced water (approximately)
FILLING
12 spinach leaves, washed and stalks removed
15 g butter
3 spring onions, finely chopped
350 g ricotta cheese
300 g sour cream
2 tablespoons self-raising flour
3 eggs
½ cup flaked almonds

1 Sift flour into a basin. Mix in wheatgerm and make a well in the centre. Add butter using fingertips. Rub butter into flour for 2 minutes or until mixture resembles a fine crumbly texture. Add enough iced water and mix using a fork until mixture forms a dough. Knead gently on a lightly floured board. Roll out pastry to fit a greased deep, 20 cm spring-form tin. Cover with plastic wrap and chill in the refrigerator for 20 minutes.
2 Prepare filling while pastry is chilling. Cook spinach until tender. Drain and cool. Squeeze out excess liquid and chop finely.
3 Melt butter in small pan. Add spring onions and cook over a gentle heat until soft. Combine ricotta cheese, sour cream, flour and eggs and beat until thick and creamy. Stir in spring onions and spinach. Cover mixture with plastic wrap and refrigerate until needed.
4 Remove pastry-lined flan tin from refrigerator. Line pastry with greaseproof paper, weighed down with rice or dried beans. Bake at 200°C for 20 minutes. Remove from oven, and remove paper and rice or beans. Leave to cool.

5 Spread filling across the base of the crust. Place the flan tin on a flat baking tray. Bake at 180°C for 30–40 minutes. Sprinkle over almonds half-way through the baking time. Serve warm, cut into wedges.

Lentil Nut Loaf with Red Capsicum Sauce

A combination of red lentils and ground nuts produce a firm savoury loaf that cuts and carries well. Eaten hot or cold, it is an excellent picnic food. The loaf and sauce can be cooked the day before required.

PREPARATION TIME: *30 minutes*
COOKING TIME: *35 minutes*
SERVES 4–6

1 cup red lentils
1 teaspoon olive oil
1 large onion, chopped
1 cup ground hazelnuts
½ cup tomato purée
¼ cup chopped basil
4 small tomatoes, peeled and sliced
60 g grated Romano cheese
1 cup wholegrain breadcrumbs
SAUCE
1 tablespoon olive oil
1 clove crushed garlic
2 red capsicums, chopped
3 ripe tomatoes, peeled, seeded and chopped

1 Place lentils in a pan and cover with cold water. Bring to the boil, reduce heat and cover and simmer until lentils are tender. Drain well.
2 Heat oil in a pan. Add onion and cook over gentle heat until it is soft. Combine onion and lentils, ground hazelnuts, tomato purée and basil. Spoon the mixture into a greased and lined 20 × 10 cm loaf tin. Cover with sliced tomatoes, cheese and breadcrumbs.
3 Bake at 180°C for 30–35 minutes.
4 Prepare sauce while loaf is baking. Heat oil in pan, add garlic and cook over a low heat for 2–3 minutes. Add capsicums and tomatoes. Cook until mixture thickens.
5 Serve hot or cold, with sauce.

Lentils have been grown for thousands of years, making them one of the oldest cultivated crops. They are high in fibre, and come in red, yellow green and brown. The red don't require soaking; the yellow, green and brown take longer to become tender. Lentils are prepared in various ways around the world. Although originally from the eastern Mediterranean countries, they are found through Europe, the Middle East and India, and are fast becoming popular in Western countries.

Butterhead lettuce, also known as butter lettuce, is one of the main varieties of lettuce available on the market today. Butterhead lettuce leaves are a soft green colour with a delicate yellow tinge on the ends. The leaves are loose, slightly curly at the ends but not as crisp as the iceburg lettuce; they just melt in your mouth. Butterhead lettuce keeps best wrapped in damp tea-towel and stored in the refrigerator.

Zucchini and Cheese Pie

Zucchini and Cheese Pie

As you are placing the squares of pastry in a round dish, change the angle of each sheet so as to create a complete cover.

PREPARATION TIME: *30 minutes*
COOKING TIME: *30 minutes*
SERVES 4–6

4 large zucchini, coarsely grated
250 g feta cheese
250 g ricotta cheese
2 tablespoons chopped mint
8 sheets filo pastry
2 tablespoons olive oil
1 tablespoon poppy seeds

1 Combine zucchini with cheeses and mint. Mix using a wooden spoon.
2 Brush each sheet of filo with oil and fold in half to form a smaller rectangle. Place one sheet in a well-oiled 23 cm pie plate, brush with oil, then top with a second sheet. Spread over one third of the filling. Repeat until all of the pastry and filling has been used, finishing with a sheet of pastry. Brush the top with oil and sprinkle with poppy seeds.
3 Bake at 200°C for 10 minutes, then reduce heat to 180°C and cook for a further 20 minutes, or until pastry is crisp and golden. Serve in wedges.

Apple and Camembert Tart

What could be tastier but apple and cheese baked in a crispy nut base. Rice cakes are available from most supermarkets. Leave the rind on the Camembert. Hazelnuts can be used in place of brazil nuts. You will need an electric blender or food processor for this recipe.

PREPARATION TIME: *35 minutes*
COOKING TIME: *40 minutes*
SERVES 8

CRUST
150 g finely chopped brazil nuts
3 rice cakes, crushed
½ cup fresh breadcrumbs
60 g butter, softened
FILLING
2 × 150 g Camembert cheeses
300 g ricotta cheese
2 eggs
1 cup low-fat reduced cream
1 large Golden Delicious apple, peeled and cut into 12 wedges

1 Combine brazil nuts, crushed rice cakes and breadcrumbs. Add softened butter and mix to combine. Press into a well-greased 23 cm fluted flan tin or pie plate. Refrigerate whilst preparing filling.
2 Cut one Camembert into thin slices. Place remaining Camembert into the bowl of the food processor and process on high for 2 minutes. Add ricotta cheese, eggs and reduced cream. Process until mixture is thick and creamy.
3 Pour cheese mixture into the chilled crust. Top with apple and Camembert slices. Bake at 180°C for 40–45 minutes. The pie is best left to cool to room temperature before cutting into wedges and serving.
Note: This tart is very rich. Serve small thin slices with crisp green salad and crusty bread. This Apple and Camembert Tart can also be used in place of the cheese course when entertaining. Serve only a very small wedge, add a few crisp apple slices. New season pears can replace apple when baking the tart.

Above: Apple and Camembert Tart. Below: Spinach Cheesecake (page 73)

The history of spices has been well recorded as far back as ancient times. They were as sought after as precious gems and minerals, and provided wealth and power, not only to the trader but to the empires that controlled them. The spices available to us today are many and varied and are as close as any supermarket shelf. They come in dried form, either whole or ground. They do have a shelf life and should be used within a reasonable time. A good guide to this is the aroma of the spice — if it has dulled it will be an indication that it is stale. Purchase in small quantities and store in small containers away from direct light.

Chillies, both red and green, have become very popular in our cuisine due to the interest in foods from countries that traditionally use them. They are used in cooking as condiments, garnishes and flavourings, and in oils and vinegars. They can be purchased fresh, dried, whole or ground. Care must be taken when preparing chillies. It is best to wear rubber gloves and keep your hands away from your face.

Eggplant Terrine

A most impressive, simply prepared recipe.

PREPARATION TIME: *1 hour*
COOKING TIME: *40 minutes*
SERVES 4–6

🌿🌿

2 eggplants, thinly sliced
2 tablespoons olive oil
2 teaspoons oil, extra
15 g butter
1¼ cups rice
2½ cups water
125 g grated Gouda cheese
½ cup grated fresh Parmesan
SAUCE
1 teaspoon olive oil, extra
1 onion, finely chopped
1 can tomatoes, chopped, liquid reserved
1 teaspoon brown sugar
2 teaspoons red wine vinegar
2 tablespoons chopped basil

1 Sprinkle eggplant slices with salt. Place in a colander and let stand for 30 minutes.
2 Whilst eggplants are being purged of their bitter juices, prepare filling. Heat oil and butter in a pan. Add rice and stir to coat the grains. Add water and bring slowly to the boil. Reduce heat to a simmer, cover and cook for 15 minutes or until rice is tender. Stir in cheeses, cover.
3 Rinse eggplant under cold running water, then pat dry with absorbent paper. Brush a large ovenproof dish with oil. Place eggplant in the dish in a single layer. Brush top with oil. Bake at 180°C for 15 minutes. Remove and allow to cool.
4 Grease a 21 × 9 cm loaf tin and line with baking paper. Over paper, line the base and sides of the tin with the cooked eggplant slices, overlapping them slightly. Reserve some slices for the top of the terrine. Fill with rice mixture, using the back of a spoon to pack it down. Cover the top with eggplant slices.
5 Cover terrine with greased aluminium foil. Sit the dish in a pan of hot water. Bake at 180°C for 35–40 minutes.
6 Prepare sauce whilst terrine is cooking. Heat oil in a small pan. Add onion and cook over a low heat for 2–3 minutes. Add tomatoes, reserved liquid, brown sugar and vinegar. Cook, uncovered, for 10 minutes. Stir in chopped basil.

7 Remove cooked terrine from oven. Turn terrine out, cool to room temperature. Slice and serve with the tomato sauce.

Spiced Potato Pancake

Rice flour and coconut milk are used to make this a thin, tender pancake. The pancake is browned on one side only, which becomes the outside of the pancake when filling. The potatoes must be cooked gently covered to prevent the spices burning and becoming bitter.

PREPARATION TIME: *30 minutes*
COOKING TIME: *15 minutes*
SERVES 4–6

🌿

PANCAKE
1 cup rice flour
1¾ cups coconut milk
1 egg
FILLING
1 tablespoon vegetable oil
2 teaspoons freshly grated ginger
⅓ cup shredded coconut
2 teaspoons cumin seeds
2 teaspoons mustard seeds
1 teaspoon turmeric
6 potatoes, peeled and diced
¼ cup water

1 Sift flour into a large bowl. Combine coconut milk and egg. Make a well in the centre of the flour, and add milk and egg mixture. Beat with a wooden spoon until well-combined and smooth.
2 Brush a pancake pan with oil. Place over a medium heat and pour in just enough batter to cover the base of the pan. Cook until mixture is set and the underside is golden brown. Continue in this manner until all mixture has been used. Stack pancakes and keep warm.
3 To prepare Filling: Heat oil in large, shallow pan over a low heat. Add ginger, coconut and spices. Cook for 3 minutes, stirring constantly. Add potatoes, then cover and cook over a low heat until potatoes are tender.
4 Fill warm pancakes with the hot potato mixture. Fold over or roll up. Serve immediately with a spicy mint relish.

Above: Eggplant Terrine. Below: Individual Olive and Tomato Pies (page 72)

EXCITING EXTRAS

Memorable meals can depend on a single dish. The secret of success of that dish can lie with the complementary sauces, relishes, flavoured butters, chutneys and salsas served alongside the meal. The following versatile 'extras' are tempting additions to any of the recipes in Vegetarian Cooking. The flavours, colours and textures of these adaptable sideliners will complete and complement any foods they accompany. They are all quick and easy to make and are well worth having on hand when planning a meal. Each recipe serves six generously. Some can be made in advance and stored, covered in the refrigerator.

Spicy Salsa

Tangy and spicy this salsa is great to pep up a dish.

PREPARATION TIME: *10 minutes*
COOKING TIME: *Nil*
SERVES 6

❧

2 small cucumbers
2 small red chillies
shredded lime rind
1 tablespoon lime juice
2 teaspoons olive oil
freshly ground pepper

1 Peel cucumbers, cut them in half lengthwise, use a small spoon to remove seeds, discard. Finely chop cucumber flesh.
2 Finely chop red chillies (include seeds if you really like it hot). Combine cucumbers and chillies in a small bowl, add shredded lime rind, lime juice, olive oil and pepper to taste.

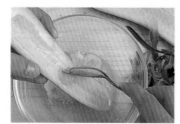

Use a small teaspoon to remove the seeds from the halved cucumbers.

Spiced Yoghurt Raita

This spicy, soothing raita is a good accompaniment to vegetable and nut curries.

PREPARATION TIME: *10 minutes*
COOKING TIME: *3 minutes*
SERVES 6

❧

15 g unsalted butter or ghee
3 cloves garlic, crushed
2 teaspoons grated fresh ginger
1 teaspoon cumin seeds
1 teaspoon black mustard seeds
½ teaspoon turmeric
1 small red chilli, finely chopped
1¼ cups natural yoghurt
1 tablespoon chopped coriander

1 Heat butter in small pan, add garlic and ginger, cook over a low heat stirring for 1 minute. Add cumin and mustard seeds, turmeric and chilli, cook stirring for 2 minutes.
2 Stir spice mixture into yoghurt, add coriander. Serve chilled.

Cook garlic, ginger, cumin seeds, mustard seeds, tumeric and chilli.

Fresh Tomato Relish

This deeply flavoured relish can be served alongside any of the vegetable fritters, lentil and bean patties. The Fresh Tomato Relish will keep for up to three days in the refrigerator.

PREPARATION TIME: *20 minutes*
COOKING TIME: *Nil*
SERVES 6

1 tablespoon olive oil
1 small red onion, finely chopped
3 ripe tomatoes, peeled and chopped
½ cup red wine vinegar
2 teaspoons brown sugar
2 zucchini, chopped
1 green capsicum, chopped
½ cup black olives, pitted, chopped
1 tablespoon capers
2 tablespoons pine nuts
2 tablespoons finely chopped flat-leaved parsley

1 Heat oil in a large pan, add onion, cover and cook over a low heat for 1 minute. Add tomatoes, cover and cook over low heat until tomatoes are soft. Add vinegar and brown sugar, simmer uncovered for about 10 minutes or until sauce has reduced and is thick.
2 Add zucchini and capsicum, cover, cook until vegetables are just tender. Cool for 10 minutes, add olives, capers, pine nuts and parsley, mix well.

Cut base of each tomato, cover with boiling water, drain, peel.

Onion Confit

The flavour of this condiment is slightly sweet and sour, it transforms dishes such as pancakes and vegetable fritters. Serve warm or at room temperature. It can be refrigerated for up to three days.

PREPARATION TIME: *15 minutes*
COOKING TIME: *35 minutes*
SERVES 6

3 medium sized brown onions
1 tablespoon olive oil
15 g unsalted butter
2 tablespoons brown sugar
1 tablespoon malt vinegar
1 tablespoon sweet white wine

1 Peel the onions and slice thinly from top to base to give short curved slices.
2 Heat oil and butter in a heavy-based pan over low heat, add onions and cook stirring occasionally until soft and wilted, about 30 minutes (the heat must be quite low, the onions must not colour).
3 Add brown sugar to pan, stir constantly until dissolved, add the vinegar and white wine, raise heat to medium, cook stirring for 1 minute. Serve cool to warm.

Cook onions over a low heat until soft and wilted but not coloured.

Sweet Capsicum and Olive Relish

This colourful side dish is perfect with vegetable terrines and teams beautifully with breads and fresh, crisp vegetables.

PREPARATION TIME: *10 minutes*
+ 1 hour standing
COOKING TIME: *Nil*
SERVES 6

1 small red capsicum
1 small green capsicum
¼ cup pitted, finely chopped black olives
¼ cup finely chopped pimento stuffed olives
2 cloves garlic, crushed
2 teaspoons dried oregano
¼ cup olive oil
1 tablespoon balsamic vinegar
freshly ground pepper

1 Chop finely the red and green capsicum. Combine capsicum, olives, garlic, oregano, oil, vinegar and pepper. Stand covered at room temperature for up to 1 hour before serving.
Note: If balsamic vinegar is unavailable use white wine vinegar. Before serving strain off oil and vinegar, if desired.

Combine the red and green capsicum, olives, garlic and oregano.

Fresh Salad &
Vegetable
Accompaniments

HERE WE PRESENT THE freshest ideas for salad and vegetable dishes. All are quick and easy to prepare, some of them like the Red Capsicum and Olive Salad or Asparagus in Lemon Sauce make ideal starters. Others such as the Artichoke and Bean Salad or Carrot and Cheese Bake can be the feature of a light meal.

Use the best seasonal salad greens and vegetables. Buying in season means you get the best produce at the best price, so choose your recipe accordingly.

Above: Red Capsicum and Olive Salad (page 83). Below: Asparagus Bean and Pine Nut Salad (page 82)

Fresh coriander can be easily recognised by its pungent, fresh aroma. The foliage is feathery and fan-like and is always purchased with the roots intact. It is most commonly used in Asian and Indian cookery. It adds a fragrant flavour to curries, rice and chutneys, and is most often used with other flavourings such as ginger, garlic, lemon and coconut. All of the plant can be used depending on the recipe. The foliage bruises easily so always wash and dry gently.

Walnut and Herb Salad

This is a crisp, refreshing combination of salad leaves and fresh herbs. Walnut halves should be of the best quality so as not to impart a bitter flavour to the salad. Walnut oil is made from grinding the walnuts to a paste and extracting the oil. It is only used as a flavouring for dressing, not for general cooking.

PREPARATION TIME: *15 minutes*
COOKING TIME: *Nil*
SERVES 4-6

1 butter lettuce
1 mignonette lettuce
½ bunch watercress
1 bunch fresh oregano
1 bunch fresh basil
½ bunch fresh mint
½ bunch fresh coriander
1 cup walnut halves
DRESSING
¼ cup tarragon vinegar
2 tablespoons walnut oil
½ teaspoon freshly ground pepper

1 Wash lettuces and watercress and dry thoroughly. Prepare herbs by breaking into sprigs or removing leaves from tough stalks. Wash and dry thoroughly.

Walnut and Herb Salad

2 Arrange lettuce, watercress and herbs in a large salad bowl. Add walnuts and toss to combine.
3 Prepare the dressing by combining all ingredients in a small bowl and whisking to combine.
4 Pour dressing over salad just prior to serving.

Asparagus, Bean and Pine Nut Salad

Pine nuts are best toasted by placing them in a slow oven for 8–10 minutes. Cover the salad with dressing just prior to serving.

PREPARATION TIME: *20 minutes*
COOKING TIME: *5 minutes*
SERVES 4–6

125 g green beans
125 g yellow beans
1 bunch asparagus
3 slices wholegrain bread
3 tablespoons olive oil
1 cos lettuce
½ cup pine nuts, toasted
½ cup grated Parmesan cheese
DRESSING
2 tablespoons olive oil
2 tablespoons cider vinegar
1 egg yolk
1 clove garlic, crushed

1 Cut beans and asparagus into 5 cm long pieces. Cook for 2 minutes in a large quantity of boiling water. Drain and plunge into iced water. Drain again and wrap in a clean tea-towel. Refrigerate until required.
2 Remove crusts from bread and cut into 1 cm squares. Heat oil in a frying pan, add bread and fry until they are golden brown on both sides. Drain on absorbent paper.
3 Wash and dry lettuce. Arrange on a large platter. Combine beans, asparagus, croutons, pine nuts and Parmesan cheese. Place on top of the lettuce.
4 Combine all ingredients for the dressing in a screw-top jar. Shake well and pour over salad. Serve immediately.

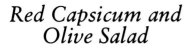
Red Capsicum and Olive Salad

This Italian-inspired salad teams very well with any pasta dish and would make an ideal starter to any meal. Capsicums can be prepared up to three days before required, covered with olive oil and kept in the refrigerator.

PREPARATION TIME: *25 minutes*
COOKING TIME: *25 minutes*
SERVES 4

❦

4 large red capsicums
2 white onions, cut into thin wedges
125 g green olives
1 tablespoon olive oil
1 tablespoon red wine vinegar
125 g piece fresh Parmesan cheese
freshly ground pepper

1 Cut capsicums in half lengthways. Remove seeds and white membrane. Place on the griller tray, skin-side up and grill on high until the skin has blistered and blackened. Using tongs remove capsicums from griller and place inside a plastic bag. Twist to secure and leave to cool. Remove from plastic bag and peel off skin. Cut capsicum into thin strips.
2 Arrange capsicum, onions and olives on serving plate. Combine olive oil and vinegar and pour over vegetables.
3 Using a potato peeler, cut off shavings of Parmesan and lay over capsicum mixture. Shake some freshly ground black pepper over the cheese and serve with crusty bread.

Beetroot Salad

Choose medium-sized, fresh, firm beet-root for this recipe. The salad is best served on the day it's made, at room temperature.

PREPARATION TIME: *25 minutes*
COOKING TIME: *Nil*
SERVES 4–6

❦

3 whole fresh beetroot, peeled and grated
2 large carrots, peeled and grated
⅓ cup orange juice
2 teaspoons grated orange rind
1 tablespoon tahini paste
½ small red chilli, finely chopped
1 tablespoon toasted sesame seeds

1 Combine grated beetroot and carrot in a large bowl.
2 Combine orange juice, rind, tahini paste and chilli in a small bowl. Mix well using a wire whisk.
3 Pour dressing over beetroot. Toss well, and serve sprinkled with sesame seeds.

Artichoke and Bean Salad

This is an easy and quick-to-prepare salad that uses both fresh and canned vegetables. Artichoke hearts can be purchased in cans or glass jars, preserved in brine or oil and vinegar dressing. Either can be used for this recipe. Add black or green olives if desired.

PREPARATION TIME: *15 minutes*
COOKING TIME: *4 minutes*
SERVES 4

❦

125 g fresh green beans, sliced
375 g artichoke hearts, well drained
1 green capsicum, sliced
2 Spanish onions, sliced thinly
3 tablespoons white wine vinegar
1 tablespoon olive oil
2 teaspoons French seeded mustard
¼ cup chopped chives

1 Cook green beans in a small amount of boiling water until just cooked. Drain and chill.
2 Combine green beans, artichoke hearts, capsicum and onions in a large bowl.
3 Combine vinegar, olive oil and mustard in a small jar and shake to combine.
4 Pour the dressing over the vegetables and toss gently. Transfer the vegetables to a large serving platter. Sprinkle with chopped chives and serve with crusty bread.

In the marketplace we see two very different types of artichokes: the globe is the most common. It is the leafy bud from a plant that is a member of the thistle family. The other type, the Jerusalem artichoke is very different as it is a tuber and resembles fresh root ginger. The two artichokes have different flavours and are prepared differently. Both are best served simply without too many other flavours — just some butter, lemon and freshly ground black pepper, which will enhance the vegetable's unique taste.

Recognised as the most cooling and refreshing of all vegetables, the cucumber has come a long way from the salad bowl. It has a delicate and distinctive flavour which is noticeable whether served hot or cold. There are a few varieties available to us, some being large green cucumbers, small crunchy Lebanese cucumbers, round white or golden cucumbers known as apple cucumbers and the delicate smooth-skinned English cucumber. The basic preparation of the cucumber depends on the type you are using and what it is being used for. They can be peeled, deseeded and salted down to remove excess moisture if they are to be combined with yoghurt or sour cream, sliced in rings for salads or cut into thin strips for stir fries or pickles.

Tomato Cucumber and Mint Salad

Choose small, firm tomatoes of equal size for this recipe. Remember to remove their cores after cutting them into quarters. Lemon can be used in place of lime.

PREPARATION TIME: *15 minutes*
COOKING TIME: *Nil*
SERVES 4–6

🌿

6 small tomatoes, cut into quarters
3 Lebanese cucumbers, peeled thinly and cut into 2.5 cm pieces
1 cup small mint leaves
1 tablespoon lime juice
DRESSING
⅔ cup plain low-fat yoghurt
1 teaspoon lime rind
1 tablespoon lime juice
1 teaspoon freshly grated ginger

1 Arrange tomatoes, cucumber and mint leaves on a large serving platter. Drizzle over lime juice. Place in the refrigerator to chill.
2 To make Dressing: Combine yoghurt, rind, juice and ginger in a small bowl. Whisk to mix well. Place into a small serving bowl.
3 Serve salad accompanied by yoghurt dressing.

Cauliflower and Broccoli Salad

This is a salad to serve in winter when cauliflower and broccoli are at their best. This dish can also be served hot, coating the vegetables with the dressing just prior to serving. This recipe is an excellent side dish to the Potato and Onion Tart (see page 60).

PREPARATION TIME: *20 minutes*
COOKING TIME: *2–3 minutes*
SERVES 4–6

½ small cauliflower
300 g broccoli
DRESSING
2 tablespoons malt vinegar
2 tablespoons olive oil
2 tablespoons light soy sauce
2 tablespoons lemon juice
1 tablespoon honey
2 tablespoons poppy seeds

1 Cut cauliflower and broccoli into florets. Place in a large pan of boiling water and cook for 2–3 minutes. Drain immediately, then place into a basin of cold water and leave for 3–4 minutes. Drain, and remove any excess moisture.
2 Combine dressing ingredients in a small bowl or jar and mix well.
3 Arrange prepared cauliflower and broccoli on a large serving plate. Pour dressing over and serve.

Endive and Grape Salad

In this very simple salad the slightly bitter curly endive and the wonderfully sweet grapes combine to give a refreshing taste.

PREPARATION TIME: *15 minutes*
COOKING TIME: *Nil*
SERVES 4–6

½ head endive, well washed and dried
200 g seedless green grapes
200 g black grapes
1 Spanish onion, chopped
DRESSING
3 tablespoons red wine vinegar
3 tablespoons olive oil
1 teaspoon French mustard
freshly ground pepper

1 Tear the endive leaves into pieces. Remove grapes from their stalks. Place endive, grapes and onion in a large serving bowl.
2 Mix vinegar, olive oil, mustard and black pepper in a small jar. Shake well until combined.
3 Pour dressing over salad and toss gently to combine. Serve.

Clockwise from top: Artichoke and Bean Salad, Beetroot Salad (page 83) and Tomato, Cucumber and Mint Salad

Cabbage and Water Chestnut Braise

This stir-fried dish can either be served as an accompaniment or as a complete meal with steamed brown or white rice, or tender egg noodles. If a thicker sauce is preferred, simply add a teaspoonful of cornflour blended with a small amount of water to the vegetables and stock. Mix well and bring to the boil until sauce thickens, then serve.

PREPARATION TIME: *15 minutes*
COOKING TIME: *10 minutes*
SERVES 4–6

1 tablespoon vegetable oil
100 g raw cashews
4 spring onions, cut into 1 cm pieces
6 Chinese dried mushrooms, soaked, stalks removed and sliced
1 cup water chestnuts, sliced
½ Chinese cabbage, shredded
¾ cup vegetable stock
⅓ cup soy sauce
2 tablespoons sweet sherry

1 Heat oil in a large shallow pan. Add cashews and cook over a medium heat until they are golden brown. Remove and set aside.
2 Add spring onions, mushrooms and water chestnuts to pan. Cook over a medium heat, stirring, for 2–3 minutes. Add cabbage and cook, stirring, for 3–4 minutes until cabbage is a bright green colour.
3 Combine stock, soy sauce and sherry and add to pan. Cook on high for 2–3 minutes. Add cashews, shaking pan to combine. Transfer to a large serving plate, serve immediately.

Using fresh herbs is becoming easier now that they are more readily available through greengrocers. Herbs are usually sold in bunches and often we cannot use all of them before they spoil. In the short term, herbs can be successfully stored for 3–4 days wrapped in aluminium foil and kept in the crisper section of your refrigerator. For longer periods, they can be frozen, either whole or just the leaves.
When required, the desired amount can be crumbled between your fingers and added to the dish.

Stir-Fried Eggs and Vegetables

In this dish, the eggs are not stirred while cooking, but gently folded and rolled to form large segments of egg and vegetable mixture. Choose a heavy-based, large, shallow pan to ensure even cooking.

PREPARATION TIME: *15 minutes*
COOKING TIME: *10 minutes*
SERVES 4–6

2 teaspoons vegetable oil
1 clove garlic, crushed
1 onion, finely chopped
1 green capsicum, finely chopped
125 g button mushrooms, sliced
1 cup mung bean sprouts
½ cup grated carrot
8 large eggs
1 tablespoon low-salt soy sauce
SAUCE
1 teaspoon cornflour
1 tablespoon soy sauce
½ cup vegetable stock
2 teaspoons sesame oil

1 Heat oil in a large, shallow pan. Add garlic, onion and capsicum. Cook over a gentle heat until the onion and capsicum are soft. Add mushrooms, mung beans and carrot. Stir over a medium heat for 2 minutes.
2 Beat eggs and soy sauce until completely combined. Pour the egg mixture into the pan. Cook, folding the mixture continuously, until eggs are just set.
3 To prepare Sauce: Blend the cornflour, soy, vegetable stock and sesame oil in a small pan. Cook over a medium heat, stirring constantly, until the sauce boils and thickens.
4 Serve a portion of egg mixture, accompanied by sauce and steamed rice, if desired.
Note: For more zest add finely shredded fresh green or red chilli, to vegetable mixture. Use gloves when working with chillies and wash gloves and hands afterwards with soap and water. Finely shredded ginger is also good to add to this dish, to shred ginger, peel and slice very thinly. Stack three or four slices together and cut into very fine shreds.

Asparagus in Lemon Sauce

Fresh, tender asparagus covered with a light, lemon sauce and topped with crunchy toasted almonds — who could resist! Asparagus is one of the most appropriate dishes to start any meal. This recipe can also be served as a light luncheon accompanied by fresh crunchy bread and salad.

PREPARATION TIME: *20 minutes*
COOKING TIME: *10 minutes*
SERVES 6

3 bunches fresh asparagus, trimmed
30 g butter
1 tablespoon plain flour
¾ cup water
⅓ cup lemon juice
2 teaspoons finely grated lemon rind
1 egg yolk
⅓ cup whole blanched almonds, toasted
(see Note)

1 Place prepared asparagus in a large shallow pan of simmering water. Cook uncovered for 10 to 12 minutes. Drain on absorbent paper before using.
2 Melt butter in a small pan. When butter has melted add flour, cook stirring for 1 minute. Remove from heat and gradually add water. Return to heat and stir constantly until the mixture boils and thickens. Remove from heat and whisk in combined lemon juice, rind and egg yolk. Return to heat and stir over a gentle heat for 3–4 minutes.
3 Arrange asparagus on one large platter or individual serving plates and pour over lemon sauce. Garnish with toasted almonds and serve.
Note: To toast almonds place them on a baking tray and cook in a preheated moderate oven 180°C for about 4 minutes or until lightly golden. Remove from oven and cool.

Almonds can also be browned in the microwave oven. Spread almonds over a micro-safe plate and cook on High 100% power until lightly golden, about 1½ minutes.

Fresh lime juice or orange juice and rind can be used in place of lemon if available.

Place prepared asparagus in shallow pan of simmering water, cook until tender.

Melt butter in small pan, add plain flour, stir well to mix. Cook for 1 minute.

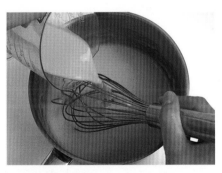

Remove from heat, stir in combined lemon juice, rind and egg yolk.

Fresh asparagus is very simply prepared. Wash the spears gently in cold running water. Break off the bottom of each spear at the point where they snap easily. If the base seems woody, trim it using a small sharp knife. Asparagus can be cooked in a pan especially made for the purpose of cooking asparagus or just as successfully in a wide shallow pan of simmering water or in a covered container in the microwave oven. Whichever method you choose, cook until the spears are just tender and be careful not to overcook, otherwise they will become tough and stringy. Asparagus can be served hot, warm or cold.

Asparagus in Lemon Sauce

Above: Creamy Coconut Vegetables. Below: Carrot and Cheese Bake

Creamy Coconut Vegetables

A combination of vegetables cooked until just tender in coconut milk, flavoured with lime and topped with coconut cream makes a refreshing accompaniment to any rice or lentil dish. Coconut milk and cream are available from most supermarkets.

PREPARATION TIME: *20 minutes*
COOKING TIME: *6 minutes*
SERVES 4–6

❦

2 cups coconut milk
100 g green beans, sliced
100 g yellow squash, sliced
½ small cauliflower, cut into florets
1 large red capsicum, cut into 8 pieces
1 tablespoon lime juice
2 tablespoons coconut cream
2 teaspoons finely grated lime rind

1 In a large pan, bring coconut milk to the boil. Add prepared vegetables and return to the boil. Reduce to a simmer and cook for a further 2 minutes.
2 Add lime juice and stir to combine. Remove vegetables from coconut milk using a slotted spoon. Place in large serving bowl.
3 Spoon coconut cream on top of vegetables, scatter with rind and serve immediately.
Note: Any seasonal vegetables can be used for this recipe, try adding fresh bean sprouts, mung bean sprouts or snowpeas.

Cucumber and Fennel with Dill

Although these vegetables are usually found in the salad bowl, they taste as good served hot, especially when flavoured with fresh dill and pepper. This vegetable combination makes a refreshing accompaniment to fried food.

PREPARATION TIME: *20 minutes*
COOKING TIME: *10 minutes*
SERVES 4–6

❦

1 tablespoon olive oil
1 fennel bulb, washed, trimmed and sliced
1 large cucumber, peeled, halved, seeds removed and sliced
⅓ cup chopped dill
freshly ground pepper
60 g roasted hazelnuts, roughly chopped

1 Heat oil in a large shallow pan. Add fennel, then cover and cook over a gentle heat until it is just tender.
2 Add cucumber and cook over a gentle heat for 3–4 minutes. Scatter dill over, and some freshly ground pepper. Shake pan to combine.
3 Place on a serving plate, garnished with roasted hazelnuts. Serve.

Carrot and Cheese Bake

Gruyère is a strong flavoured Swiss cheese. Other Swiss cheese such as Gouda, may be substituted.

PREPARATION TIME: *20 minutes*
COOKING TIME: *15 minutes*
SERVES 4–6

❦

6 large carrots, sliced
½ cup vegetable stock
½ cup white wine
2 spring onions, sliced
2 tablespoons lemon juice
1 teaspoon grated lemon rind
3 eggs, lightly beaten
125 g grated Gruyère cheese
½ cup finely chopped parsley

1 Place carrots, vegetable stock, white wine, spring onions, lemon juice and rind into a pan. Bring slowly to the boil, reduce to a simmer and cook until carrots are just tender.
2 Transfer carrots to a bowl. Add eggs, cheese and parsley. Mix well to combine.
3 Pour carrot mixture into a well-greased 20 cm springform tin. Bake at 180°C for 20–25 minutes or until custard has set.
4 Remove from oven, cool slightly. Release base from tin, cut into wedges and serve.

Limes are the bright-green skinned fruit from the citrus family. They have bright green flesh that produces a refreshing, tart juice when squeezed. The rind of the lime is very fine and care must be taken when grating so as not to include the bitter white pith which lies just under the skin. Limes and lemons can be substituted for each other with only a slight variation of flavour.

Curry powder is most probably the world's earliest spice blend. Although many varieties of prepared curry powders can be purchased, many people blend their own. Curry powder can be a blend of as many as 60 spices and herbs. The basic spices used are turmeric, fenugreek, cumin, coriander and chilli. The amounts and proportions vary depending on requirements and personal taste. The turmeric supplies the yellow colour and a slight sweetness: fenugreek, cumin and coriander supply the aromatic flavour; and the chilli, of course, gives a dish the heat. Curry powder is best made in small amounts and kept in a sealed glass jar away from direct light. The powder can also be made into a paste by the addition of a small amount of oil. Curry paste is best kept in the refrigerator.

Sesame Pumpkin

In this recipe, the sweet, nutty flavour of pumpkin is enhanced by the addition of the Asian-style coating. Choose whatever variety of pumpkin that you prefer.

PREPARATION TIME: *15 minutes*
COOKING TIME: *20 minutes*
SERVES 6

12 serving size pieces pumpkin
½ cup light soy sauce
½ teaspoon sesame oil
2 teaspoons honey
1 spring onion, sliced
2 tablespoons sesame seeds

1 Arrange pumpkin pieces in a single layer in a shallow oven-proof dish.
2 Combine soy sauce, sesame oil, honey, spring onion and sesame seeds in a small pan. Cook over gentle heat, stirring constantly, until the honey has melted and the mixture is completely combined.
3 Pour soy mixture over pumpkin, ensuring that pumpkin pieces are well coated. Bake at 200°C for 20–30 minutes, turning once during baking. Serve immediately.
Note: If desired sweet potato can replace the pumpkin in this recipe. A squeeze of orange juice and finely grated orange rind will add extra sweetness, add the juice and rind to pumpkin about 10 minutes before end of cooking time.

Mushroom and Wheat Salad

Burghul, or cracked wheat which is slightly coarser than burghul, is used extensively throughout the Middle East, especially in Lebanon where it is used in the making of the very popular tabbouli salad. Soak burghul in hot or cold water until soft before cooking. Rinse and squeeze excess water from burghul.

PREPARATION TIME: *30 minutes*
COOKING TIME: *Nil*
SERVES 4–6

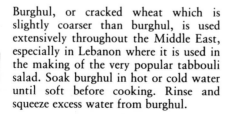

1 cup burghul wheat
200 g button mushrooms, sliced
1 small red capsicum, chopped
½ bunch chives, chopped
DRESSING
2 tablespoons lemon juice
2 tablespoons olive oil
1 clove garlic, crushed
1 teaspoon finely chopped ginger
½ teaspoon freshly ground pepper

1 Place burghul into a bowl, cover with hot water and leave to soak for 30 minutes. Drain and squeeze excess moisture out with your hands.
2 Combine mushrooms, capsicum and chives in a large basin. Add burghul and toss to combine.
3 Combine lemon juice, olive oil, garlic, ginger and black pepper in screw-top jar and shake to combine. Pour the dressing over the salad. Chill before serving.

Curried Brussels Sprouts

Choose small, bright green sprouts with no trace of yellowing.

PREPARATION TIME: *15 minutes*
COOKING TIME: *15 minutes*
SERVES 6

750 g small Brussels sprouts
15 g butter
1 teaspoon curry paste
¼ cup lime juice
1 teaspoon finely grated lime rind
½ cup shredded coconut, toasted

1 Cook Brussels sprouts in boiling water until just tender. Drain and set aside.
2 Melt butter in a shallow pan. Add curry paste, lime juice and rind and cook over a gentle heat for 2 minutes.
3 Add cooked sprouts and toss over medium heat for 3–4 minutes until sprouts are well coated in curry mixture. Do not allow them to brown.
4 Arrange Brussels sprouts on a serving plate, and sprinkle with toasted shredded coconut. Serve immediately.

Curried Cauliflower and Potatoes

Because of the selected spices used in this recipe, the vegetables are delicately coloured and flavoured.

PREPARATION TIME: *20 minutes*
COOKING TIME: *20 minutes*
SERVES 6

30 g butter
2 teaspoons ground cumin
2 teaspoons ground coriander
1 teaspoon garam masala
1 teaspoon turmeric
½ teaspoon dried chilli powder
2 tomatoes, peeled and chopped
4 large potatoes, peeled and cubed
½ cauliflower, cut into florets
1 cup cooked chick peas
½ cup water
2 tablespoons lemon juice
1 teaspoon grated lemon rind
1 cup plain yoghurt
½ cup fresh coriander sprigs, for garnish

1 Heat butter in a large pan. Add combined spices and cook over a gentle heat for 1–2 minutes. Add tomatoes, stirring to combine. Add potatoes, cauliflower and chick peas, cook over a medium heat for 5 minutes.

2 Add water, lemon juice and rind, stir and reduce heat. Cover and cook over a low heat until the vegetables are tender.

3 Stir in yoghurt, being careful not to break or mash the tender vegetables. Simmer, uncovered, 2–3 minutes. Serve garnished with coriander sprigs.

Minted Peas and Mushrooms

These peas and mushrooms are cooked in a spicy tomato sauce with the added flavour boost of freshly chopped mint. Not only is it a great accompaniment to Indian-style food, but makes an excellent start to a meal, especially if topped with a spoonful of yoghurt or cottage cheese.

PREPARATION TIME: *15 minutes*
COOKING TIME: *15 minutes*
SERVES 6

1 teaspoon vegetable oil
1 clove garlic, crushed
2 teaspoons grated ginger
1 teaspoon turmeric
1 teaspoon ground coriander
1 teaspoon ground cumin
1 teaspoon garam masala
2 large ripe tomatoes, peeled and chopped
500 g snow peas
250 g button mushrooms
½ cup roughly chopped mint

1 Heat oil in large pan. Add garlic, ginger and spices and cook over a gentle heat for 2–3 minutes. Add tomatoes, stirring to combine. Cook over a low heat until the mixture thickens.

2 Add peas and simmer, uncovered, for 4 minutes. Then add mushrooms and simmer a further 5 minutes.

3 Stir in mint and cook a further 2 minutes. Transfer mixture to a large serving bowl and serve.

To obtain maximum flavour and nutrition from mushrooms, do not peel or wash them before using. Wipe gently with damp cloth and trim stalks with a sharp knife if necessary.

Minted Peas and Mushrooms

A bouquet garni is the classic flavouring for stocks, casseroles, soups, sauces and stews. A bouquet garni is made of a number of aromatic herbs tied or bagged together. The most commonly included herbs are sprig of parsley, a bay leaf and a sprig of thyme, placed in the hollow of a piece of celery and tied with string for ease of removal. Bouquets made of dried herbs can be secured in a square of muslin or cheese cloth. All bouquets are removed before puréeing or serving.

Beans and Tomato

Beans and Tomato

Smooth, white haricot beans have been used for this bean and tomato stew. This dish is an excellent accompaniment to the Zucchini Tart (see page 72).

PREPARATION TIME: *10 minutes +
6-8 hours soaking*
COOKING TIME: *1 hour*
SERVES 4–6

3 cups haricot beans
1 carrot
1 stick celery
1 sprig parsley
1 whole onion, studded with 4 cloves
1 teaspoon olive oil
2 cloves garlic, crushed
2 cans whole tomatoes, reserve liquid
¼ cup molasses
2 teaspoons Worcestershire sauce
2 teaspoons prepared French mustard

1 Place beans in a bowl. Cover with cold water and soak 6-8 hours. Drain well before using.
2 Place beans, carrot, celery, parsley and onion in a large pan. Cover with cold water and bring slowly to the boil. Reduce heat, cover and cook for 45 minutes. Drain beans, discard celery, parsley and onion.
3 Heat oil in large pan. Add garlic and cook over gentle heat for 1 minute. Add tomatoes and liquid, molasses, Worcestershire sauce and French mustard. Simmer, uncovered, for 10 minutes.
4 Add beans, cover and cook over a low heat for 10 minutes. Serve.

Spicy Potatoes and Spinach

Although orange sweet potato (known as kumara) has been used for this recipe, any potato can be substituted. Adjust the amount of chilli to suit personal taste. When cooking the spinach, the water remaining on the leaves from having washed it should be sufficient to cook it.

PREPARATION TIME: *20 minutes*
COOKING TIME: *6 minutes*
SERVES 4–6

12 spinach leaves, washed and stalks
removed
30 g butter
2 onions, sliced
2 teaspoons finely grated ginger
2 green chillies, finely chopped
1 teaspoon turmeric
1 onion, sliced
500 g orange sweet potato, peeled and
cut into thick slices
¼ cup water

1 Coarsely shred spinach, place in a pan and cover and cook over a medium heat until it is just tender. Set aside.
2 Melt butter in a large shallow pan. Add ginger, chilli and turmeric. Cook over gentle heat for 2–3 minutes. Add onion and potato, cook, shaking pan, until potato is completely coated with the butter mixture.
3 Add water, cover and cook over a low heat until potato is tender. Add spinach to pan and cook on high, shaking pan, for 2–3 minutes. Serve.
Note: For extra flavour add about 2 teaspoons of black mustard seeds with the butter and onions at the start of cooking. There are three varieties of mustard seeds, black and brown are aromatic and spicy, yellow are generally used for mustard.

Above: Spicy Potatoes and Spinach. Below: Curried Cauliflower and Potatoes (page 91)

Desserts &
Teatime Treats

SPLENDID SWEET DESSERTS and teatime treats make this chapter
special. We have included rich tarts, puddings, crumbles and
cheesecake; all will make a fabulous finale to any meal. The Apple
and Passionfruit Nut Crumble and Steamed Date and Pecan
Pudding with Orange Sauce are sure to become firm favourites.

We have added some of our best loved recipes for wholesome
muffins, most fruit filled cakes and cookies. These delightful
teatime treats are perfect for morning or afternoon tea, they can be
served with butter, ricotta cheese and fruit. All are easy to prepare,
some like the Blueberry Cheese Muffins and Apple and Currant
Cookies can be made by children are ideal for brunch or as an after
school snack.

Above: Marzipan Pear and Coconut Tart (page 96). Below: Carrot and Almond Syrup Cake with Creme Fraîche (page 96)

When a recipe stipulates a specific coarseness of semolina to be used, it is advisable to do so. (Semolina is available in three grades of coarseness: coarse, medium and fine ground.) The final result will vary considerably, and in some instances the recipe may fail altogether if the wrong grade is used. Semolina can be used as a breakfast cereal, in cakes, as a soup thickener, in breads, puddings and in the making of pasta. It is also used to make couscous, where the semolina is combined with water to form tiny pellets, which are then dried. Couscous is an ideal ingredient for vegetarian cuisine.

When making a syrup cake, it is best to *brush* the cooled cake with hot syrup or vice versa — hot cake with cooled syrup. Do not pour syrup onto the cake as it quickly settles to the base, leaving the top half of the cake dry.

Marzipan Pear and Coconut Tart

This tart makes a delicious treat for an afternoon with friends. If firm ripe pears are unavailable or too costly, try using well-drained, canned pear halves. For a more intensely coconut-flavoured base, you may wish to add a quarter teaspoon coconut essence to the butter and marzipan mixture before adding the eggs.

PREPARATION TIME: *10 minutes*
COOKING TIME: *40 minutes*
SERVES 6–8

❧

60 g butter
125 g packaged/prepared marzipan
2 tablespoons caster sugar
2 eggs
½ cup dessicated coconut
2 tablespoons ground almonds
1 cup self-raising flour, sifted
3 small firm brown fleshed pears, peeled, cored and halved
¼ cup apricot jam

1 Brush an 18 cm loose bottom fluted flan tin or a 20 cm round sandwich pan with some melted butter or oil. Line the base with greaseproof paper, then grease the paper.
2 Beat butter, marzipan and sugar in a small bowl with an electric mixer until light and fluffy. Add eggs, one at a time, beating well after each addition.
3 Add coconut, almonds and flour to the creamed mixture. Stir with a metal spoon until just combined. Spread mixture evenly over the base of prepared pan.
4 Using a sharp knife, cut each pear into 5 mm thick slices from base of pear crossways to the narrow end. Carefully lift sliced pear onto cake mixture and gently press each piece about 1 cm into the cake, maintaining the shape of the pear. Repeat with remaining pear.
5 Bake the tart at 180°C for about 35–40 minutes or until a skewer comes out clean when inserted into the centre of tart. Leave tart to cool in pan. Transfer to a serving plate and brush evenly with warmed and strained jam.
Note: Tart can be served warm if preferred, dusted lightly with icing sugar.

Carrot and Almond Syrup Cake with Crème Fraîche

A splendid combination of carrot and almond create this beautiful dessert cake drizzled with a light lemon syrup and served with crème fraîche. It makes an ideal finale to any dinner party. You can buy crème fraîche from some delicatessens or make your own the day before using the recipe below.

PREPARATION TIME: *15 minutes +
overnight refrigeration*
COOKING TIME: *45 minutes*
SERVES 10–12

❧❧

125 g butter
3 teaspoons grated lemon rind
1 cup caster sugar
4 eggs
4 cups coarsely grated carrot
1½ cups ground almonds
2 tablespoons self-raising flour
1 teaspoon baking powder
1 cup fine ground semolina
LEMON SYRUP
½ cup water
2 tablespoons lemon juice
⅔ cup sugar
CREME FRAICHE
½ cup thickened cream
½ cup buttermilk

1 Brush a 23 cm springform pan with melted butter or oil. Line the base and sides with greaseproof paper, grease paper.
2 Beat butter, rind and sugar in a small bowl until light and fluffy. Add eggs, one at a time, beating well after each addition.
3 Transfer mixture to a large mixing bowl. Using a metal spoon, fold in carrot, almonds, sifted flour, baking powder and semolina until just combined. Spread mixture evenly into prepared pan, smoothing the surface. Bake at 180°C 45 minutes or until a skewer comes out clean when inserted in centre. Remove from oven, and leave to cool in pan. Brush cooled cake generously with hot syrup. Serve cut into wedges with a spoonful of crème fraîche.
4 To make Lemon Syrup: Combine all ingredients in a small pan. Stir over a low

heat for about 5 minutes or until the sugar is dissolved. Bring to the boil, then reduce heat and simmer, uncovered for 5 minutes without stirring.

5 To make Crème Fraîche: Whisk cream in a small bowl until soft peaks form. Add buttermilk and stir. Store, covered, in refrigerator for several hours.

Note: Cake is best made and brushed with syrup on the day of serving. Crème Fraîche and Lemon Syrup can both be made a day ahead, reheat syrup to brush over cooled cake.

Apple and Passionfruit Nut Crumble

This is a delicious combination of apples and passionfruit, topped with a muesli nut crumble. Firm green pears can be used in place of apples, and almonds in place of hazelnuts. This dessert can be improved (if that's possible) by being served with a large spoonful of passionfruit yoghurt.

PREPARATION TIME: *20 minutes*
COOKING TIME: *35 minutes*
SERVES 4–6

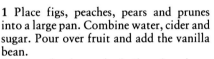

4 large cooking apples
4 large passionfruit
⅓ cup apple juice
½ cup self-raising flour
30 g butter
¾ cup natural muesli
⅓ cup chopped hazelnuts
passionfruit yoghurt, to serve

1 Peel, core, quarter and slice the apples. Place into an ovenproof glass or ceramic dish. Remove pulp from the passionfruit and spoon over the apples. Pour over apple juice.

2 Sift flour into a small bowl. Rub in the butter using your fingers, until the mixture is combined. Add muesli and hazelnuts and mix gently to combine.

3 Spoon the crumble mixture over apples. Press down gently using your hand. Bake at 180°C for 35 minutes or until the apples are tender when tested with a skewer. Serve hot or cold with a dollop of passionfruit yoghurt.

Winter Fruit Salad

Other combinations of fruits may be used, but be sure to choose fruits that will take the same time to cook. The fruit salad may be made 2–3 days before required. Serve with lightly whipped cream and small almond biscuits.

PREPARATION TIME: *15 minutes*
COOKING TIME: *30 minutes*
SERVES 4–6

200 g dried figs
100 g dried peaches
100 g dried pears
100 g dessert prunes, stones removed
2 cups water
1 cup apple cider
¼ cup raw sugar
1 vanilla bean, cut in half lengthways

1 Place figs, peaches, pears and prunes into a large pan. Combine water, cider and sugar. Pour over fruit and add the vanilla bean.

2 Bring slowly to the boil, reduce heat, and cover and simmer until fruit is tender (approximately 30 minutes).

3 Allow to cool to room temperature before serving. Remove the vanilla bean just before serving.

A dry vanilla bean, even one you have used, can be stored in your container of sugar — will impart vanilla flavour to the sugar for many months. Use the sugar when making cakes or sweet sauces and desserts.

Winter Fruit Salad

Steamed puddings can be cooked in ceramic or metal basins placed directly in simmering water or in the top section of a steamer. If cooking directly in water, the water should come halfway up the side of the pudding basin and it is a good idea to sit the basin on an old saucer or plate to prevent direct contact with the heat source. Water must always be simmering, not boiling rapidly. Water must never be allowed to come off the simmer or boil dry. To aid as a reminder, place 2 or 3 small coins into the water whilst the water is simmering. The coins will make a jingling noise whilst the water is simmering.

Apple and Currant Cookies

Apple and Currant Cookies

Apple and currant cookies will keep, stored in an airtight container, for up to one week.

PREPARATION TIME: *10 minutes*
COOKING TIME: *20 minutes*
MAKES *about 30 biscuits*

125 g butter
½ cup brown sugar
1 teaspoon imitation vanilla essence
1 egg
½ cup finely chopped pie apple
¼ cup currants
1½ cups rolled oats
1 cup wholemeal self-raising flour

1 Beat butter, sugar and essence in a small bowl with an electric mixer until light and fluffy. Add egg, beat for a further minute or until combined.
2 Add apple, currants, oats and sifted flour, including husks, to the creamed mixture. Stir to form a soft dough.
3 Drop level tablespoons of mixture onto greased oven trays, about 5 cm apart. Bake at 180°C for 12–15 minutes or until golden brown and firm.
4 Transfer cookies to a wire rack to cool.
Note: If pie apple is not available, try substituting ½ cup finely chopped dried apple that has been soaked in ⅓ cup boiling water for half an hour or until all liquid has been absorbed and apple is plump.

Steamed Date and Pecan Pudding with Orange Sauce

An easy-to-make heartwarming dessert that will quickly become a favourite with family and friends.

PREPARATION TIME: *30 minutes*
COOKING TIME: *2 hours*
SERVES *6–8*

125 g butter
1 cup caster sugar
4 eggs
2 cups dates, chopped
⅔ cup chopped pecans
¼ cup milk
1 cup self-raising flour
1 cup plain flour
1 teaspoon ground cardamom
CARDAMOM SAUCE
30 g unsalted butter
2 tablespoons brown sugar
1 teaspoon ground cardamom
¾ cup orange juice

1 Grease a six cup capacity pudding steamer with melted butter. Line base with greaseproof paper, grease paper.
2 Beat butter and sugar in a small mixer bowl until light and creamy. Add eggs gradually, beating thoroughly after each addition.
3 Transfer mixture to large bowl, fold in chopped dates, pecans and milk. Stir in sifted flours and cardamom. Stir until just combined.
4 Spoon mixture into prepared steamer, cover with a greased round of foil, secure with lid and string.
5 Carefully place steamer in a large pan of simmering water that comes half-way up the side of the steamer. Cover, cook for 2 hours. Do not let the pudding boil dry, replenish with simmering water as the pudding cooks.
6 To make Cardamom Sauce: Combine butter, brown sugar and cardamom in small pan, cook over a low heat stirring until butter melts and mixture is smooth, stir in orange juice. Serve warm over hot pudding.

Above: Steamed Date and Pecan Pudding with Orange Sauce. Below: Apple and Passionfruit Nut Crumble (page 97)

Ricotta Rolls with Apricot Sauce

These ricotta-filled pastries are perfect for a special dinner party. Filo pastry is paper thin and does require gentle handling. Be sure to keep it covered with a damp tea-towel whilst preparing this dessert.

PREPARATION TIME: *25 minutes*
COOKING TIME: *10 minutes*
SERVES 6

❧ ❧

⅓ cup currants
2 teaspoons finely grated orange rind
½ cup orange juice
200 g ricotta cheese
12 sheets filo pastry
⅔ cup low fat plain yoghurt
½ cup flaked almonds
SAUCE
425 g can apricots in nectar
2 teaspoons lemon juice
TOPPING
2 teaspoons icing sugar
1 teaspoon ground cinnamon

1 Combine currants, orange rind and juice in a small pan. Place over a low heat and allow to simmer, uncovered, until all liquid has evaporated. Allow to cool completely. Combine cooled currants with ricotta cheese.

Ricotta Rolls with Apricot Sauce

2 Spread one sheet of filo onto a flat surface. Brush with yoghurt and sprinkle with flaked almonds. Fold in half lengthways. Place a spoonful of ricotta mixture at one end. Fold over top to encase the filling, then fold in the edges and roll. Place onto a lightly greased baking tray.
3 Continue with remaining filo and ricotta in exactly the same way. Bake at 200°C for 8–10 minutes until rolls are crisp and golden.
4 Prepare sauce while rolls are cooking. Place apricots, nectar and lemon juice into a blender and blend on high until smooth. Just before serving, gently heat the sauce in a small pan.
5 When rolls are cooked, cool on a wire rack. Combine icing sugar and cinnamon and sieve over rolls. Serve rolls with warm apricot sauce.

Blueberry Cheese Muffins

Blueberries and cheese are a great combination. These muffins are so easy to prepare that children would enjoy making them. They are suitable for brunch or as an after-school snack. Fresh blueberries, if available, can be used instead of canned.

PREPARATION TIME: *10 minutes*
COOKING TIME: *20 minutes*
MAKES 12 *muffins*

❧

1 cup self-raising flour
1 cup wholemeal self-raising flour
2 tablespoons toasted muesli
½ cup caster sugar
425 g can blueberries, well drained, or
200 g punnet fresh blueberries
¾ cup creamed cottage cheese
1 egg, lightly beaten
60 g butter, melted
½ cup milk

1 Brush the base of a 12-cup muffin pan with melted butter or oil.
2 Sift flours into a large mixing bowl. Add muesli and sugar. Make a well in the centre. Add blueberries, cheese, egg, butter and milk. Using a large metal spoon, stir

ingredients quickly together until just combined. The batter will not be totally smooth at this stage but will result in a light and well-risen muffin.

3 Drop spoonfuls of the mixture into the prepared pan, filling each cup two thirds full. Do not smooth the surface.

4 Bake muffins at 200°C for 20 minutes or until golden, well-risen and cooked through. Leave to stand in the pan for 1 minute before turning out onto a wire rack to cool.

Oaty Sultana and Ginger Cake

This traditional oatmeal and ginger cake from the north of England known as Parkin, is usually served with cheese and apples. Our version of this cake incorporates the apple into the cake and is topped with a creamy cheese topping. Without the topping, this version of Oaty Sultana and Ginger Cake can be stored in the refrigerator for up to two weeks. The topping is optional.

PREPARATION TIME: *20 minutes +*
10 minutes standing
COOKING TIME: *40 minutes*
SERVES 12

❧ ❧

125 g butter
½ cup molasses
½ cup brown sugar
⅓ cup milk
1½ cups wholemeal plain flour
½ cup fine ground oatmeal
1 teaspoon bicarbonate of soda
½ teaspoon baking powder
1 teaspoon ground ginger
2 cups rolled oats
¾ cup slivered almonds
½ cup sultanas
1 cup pie-pack apple, chopped
2 tablespoons finely chopped glacé ginger
2 eggs, lightly beaten
CREAMY CHEESE TOPPING
250 g cream cheese
⅓ cup honey
2 teaspoons grated lemon rind
2 teaspoons lemon juice

1 Brush a deep, 23 cm square cake pan with some melted butter or oil. Line the base and sides with greaseproof paper and then grease the paper.

2 Stir butter, molasses and sugar in small pan over a low heat for about 5 minutes or until butter melts and sugar dissolves. Add milk and stir until combined. Remove from heat and cool slightly.

3 Sift flour, including husks, oatmeal, soda, baking powder and ground ginger into a large mixing bowl. Add oats, almonds, sultanas, apple and ginger. Stir until combined.

4 Make a well in the centre and add the cooled butter mixture and the eggs. Stir ingredients together with a wooden spoon. Spoon mixture into prepared pan and smooth surface.

5 Bake at 180°C for 40 minutes or until skewer comes out clean when inserted. Leave to stand in pan for 10 minutes before turning onto wire rack to cool. Spread with creamy cheese topping when cold.

6 To make Creamy Cheese Topping: Beat cheese and honey together in a small bowl with an electric mixer until light and fluffy. Stir in rind and juice.

Note: Oaty Sultana and Ginger Cake is best made one day ahead of serving as the flavours will develop.

Oatmeal has a high fat content and does not keep for long periods, as the fat can cause it to become rancid. Buy only what is required for the recipe. Oatmeal is available in varying grades of coarseness: coarse, medium, fine and very fine, which is like a powder. If the oatmeal you have is coarser than is required for the recipe, you can use a food processor or a grinder to grind it further.

Oaty Sultana and Ginger Cake

Above: Moist Date and Walnut Cake (page 104). Below: Pumpkin and Prune Muffins

Fruity Nut Bars

Use a selection of dried fruits of your choice.

PREPARATION TIME: *15 minutes +*
20 minutes standing
COOKING TIME: *20 minutes*
MAKES *2 bars*

½ cup finely chopped dried apricots
⅓ cup boiling water
½ cup mixed dried fruit
½ cup sultanas
½ cup currants
1 cup whole Brazil nuts
¼ cup unblanched whole almonds
1 cup white self-raising flour
1 teaspoon ground nutmeg
1 tablespoon finely grated orange rind
¼ cup golden syrup
¼ cup orange juice
2 eggs, lightly beaten

1 Brush 2, 8 × 26 cm bar pans with melted butter or oil. Line the base and sides with greaseproof paper, then grease the paper.
2 Place apricots in a small bowl, pour over boiling water, and leave to stand, covered, for 20 minutes or until almost all the liquid is absorbed and apricots are plump. Do not drain.
3 Combine undrained apricots, fruits and nuts in a large mixing bowl. Add sifted flour, spice and rind. Stir until combined.
4 Make a well in the centre and add syrup, juice and eggs. Mix well. Spoon the mixture into prepared pans, smoothing the surface with the back of a spoon or knife.
5 Bake at 180°C for 20 minutes or until golden and a skewer inserted comes out clean. Leave to stand for 5 minutes before turning out onto a rack to cool.

Pumpkin and Prune Muffins

Quick and easy-to-prepare, these muffins are moist and flavoursome. Pumpkin and prune muffins can be served hot or cold with cottage cheese.

PREPARATION TIME: *15 minutes*
COOKING TIME: *20 minutes*
MAKES *12 muffins*

1½ cups wholemeal self-raising flour
1 teaspoon mixed spice
⅓ cup rolled oats
⅔ cup brown sugar
1 cup cooked mashed pumpkin (about 350 g)
¾ cup prunes, chopped
1 egg, lightly beaten
125 g butter, melted

1 Brush base of twelve-cup muffin pan with melted butter or oil.
2 Sift flour and spice into a large mixing bowl, returning husks to the bowl. Add oats and sugar. Stir and make a well in the centre. Add pumpkin, prunes, egg and butter to bowl. Using a large metal spoon, stir quickly until ingredients are mixed.
3 Drop spoonfuls of the mixture into prepared pan, filling each cup two thirds full. Do not smooth the surface.
4 Bake muffins at 200°C for 20 minutes or until golden, well-risen and cooked through. Leave to stand in pan for 1 minute before turning out onto wire rack.

When making muffins, the ingredients should be mixed lightly and quickly to prevent over-development of the gluten which will result in a tough, porous and peaked muffin. Optimum muffins should be well-risen with a rounded, pebbled surface, symmetrical in shape, with a light, tender, golden brown crust.

Fruity Nut Bars

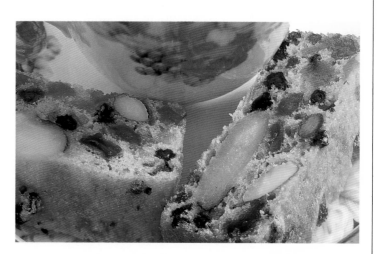

To ensure the easy removal of cakes etc. from their tins after baking, carefully line the base and sides of all cake tins, including springform pans and ring pans, with greaseproof paper and brush with melted butter or oil before filling with the mixture.

Dried dates should be soft, juicy and sticky to touch. If they are dry they are of poor quality and should be rejected. Dates are high in sugar and should be avoided if you are on a kilojoule-controlled diet. They contain vitamin A and some B vitamins. Fresh dates are also available from your greengrocer. They should be purchased when their skins are smooth and shiny brown. Dried and fresh dates are an excellent snack and dessert food served with cheese and nuts, or lashings of fresh natural yoghurt.

Moist Date and Walnut Cake

This is a delightful version of the traditional date and walnut loaf and is very rich and moist as it is made with fresh dates, molasses, glacé pineapple and walnuts. Serve it as a dessert cake with ricotta cheese, or sliced and buttered as a tea-time treat.

PREPARATION TIME: *15 minutes*
COOKING TIME: *45 minutes*
SERVES 8–10

100 g butter
1/3 cup brown sugar
1 tablespoon molasses
1 1/2 cups chopped fresh dates
2 teaspoons imitation vanilla essence
1 egg, lightly beaten
1 teaspoon bicarbonate of soda
1 cup chopped walnuts
100 g chopped glacé pineapple
2/3 cup wholemeal plain flour
1 cup white self-raising flour
1/4 cup milk

1 Brush a deep, 14 × 21cm, loaf pan with melted butter or oil. Line the base and sides with greaseproof paper, then grease the paper.
2 Stir butter, sugar and molasses in a small pan over a low heat for about 5 minutes or until butter melts and sugar dissolves. Remove from heat and stir in dates. Allow to cool slightly.
3 Add essence and egg to the date mixture. Stir in soda and mix well.
4 Place walnuts, pineapple and cooled date mixture into large mixing bowl. Sift flours, including husks, over fruit and nut mixture. Add milk, and stir with a wooden spoon until all ingredients are combined. Spoon mixture into prepared pan. Bake at 180°C for about 45 minutes or until skewer comes out clean when inserted into cake centre. Cool loaf in pan before turning out.
Note: If desired, ice moist Date and Walnut Cake with creamy cheese topping from the Oaty Sultana and Ginger Cake (see page 101).

Shredded Pastry and Custard Slice

The old-fashioned favourite Greek custard slice has been adapted slightly here, substituting filo pastry for shredded pastry.

PREPARATION TIME: *20 minutes*
COOKING TIME: *45 minutes*
SERVES 10–12

3 1/2 cups milk
1/2 cup fine ground semolina
2 tablespoons cornflour
1/2 cup caster sugar
3 eggs
2 teaspoons imitation vanilla essence
375 g packet filo pastry
60 g butter, melted
1 tablespoon oil
SYRUP
3/4 cup sugar
1/2 cup water
3 whole cloves
1/4 teaspoon rosewater

1 Heat 3 cups of the milk in a medium pan over a low heat for 10 minutes or until almost boiling. Beat semolina, cornflour, sugar, eggs and remaining milk in a small bowl with an electric mixer for 3 minutes.
2 Stir semolina mixture into hot milk. Stir over a low heat until custard boils and thickens. Remove from heat and stir in essence. Allow to cool slightly.
3 Unroll filo pastry and reroll tightly. Use a serrated knife and cut pastry into thin shreds. Place shredded pastry in a large bowl. Combine melted butter and oil and pour over pastry. Rub butter into pastry using your fingertips. Divide pastry into two equal portions, and cover one portion with plastic wrap.
4 Press one portion of pastry evenly over the base of a deep, 20 × 35 cm, ovenproof dish. Pour custard filling over pastry and smooth the surface. Roll out remaining pastry and carefully cover filling.
5 Bake custard slice at 180°C for 45 minutes or until pastry is crisp and golden. Remove from oven and leave to cool.
6 Using a sharp knife, cut slice into 12–15 pieces, but do not remove from dish at this

stage. Brush hot syrup over cooled slice and leave to cool before serving.

7 To make Syrup: Combine sugar, water and cloves in a small pan. Stir over a low heat until sugar has dissolved. Bring to the boil, reduce heat and simmer, uncovered and without stirring, for 5 minutes. Remove from heat and stir in rosewater.

Pears with Coconut Custard

A rich custard made with coconut cream and served with pears poached in a honey syrup makes a delightfully different winter dessert. Coconut cream is available in cartons and tins from most supermarkets. Choose large yellow pears that have a strong perfume, which is an indication of their ripeness.

PREPARATION TIME: *20 minutes*
COOKING TIME: *30 minutes*
SERVES 4–6

½ cup honey
1½ cups water
¼ cup lemon juice
4 large pears, peeled, cored and thickly sliced
CUSTARD
4 eggs
½ cup raw sugar
1 tablespoon cornflour
1 cup coconut cream
1 cup milk
½ cup shredded toasted coconut

1 Combine honey, water and lemon juice in a pan. Heat gently, stirring until well combined. Simmer uncovered for 3 minutes. Add pear slices and cook gently until just tender.
2 Beat eggs, sugar and cornflour together until well combined. Add coconut cream and milk. Mix well.
3 Remove pears from cooking liquid place in a shallow ovenproof dish. Pour custard mixture over pears. Place dish into a baking tray, fill with enough water to come halfway up the side of the custard-filled dish. Bake at 160°C for 30 minutes or until a knife inserted comes out clean. Remove dish from water. Sprinkle toasted coconut over custard. Serve warm.

Left: Shredded Pastry and Custard Slice.
Right: Pears with Coconut Custard.

Leftover chopped dried fruits can be combined together and stored in jars in a syrup made from honey and orange juice. Seal with a tight fitting lid and store in a cool, dark cupboard. Add macerated dried fruits to your favourite muffin, bread or fruit cake recipe.

Try grinding a stick of cinnamon to a fine powder in a coffee grinder next time cinnamon is required in a recipe. You will find freshly ground spice is more flavoursome and aromatic.

Sweet Potato Cheesecake

A luscious, baked cheesecake which is best made a day ahead. If orange sweet potato is unavailable, use pumpkin instead. Do not add butter or milk to either sweet potato or pumpkin when mashing the vegetable.

PREPARATION TIME: *20 minutes +*
overnight refrigeration
COOKING TIME: *1 hour*
SERVES 6–8

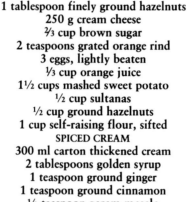

1 tablespoon finely ground hazelnuts
250 g cream cheese
⅔ cup brown sugar
2 teaspoons grated orange rind
3 eggs, lightly beaten
⅓ cup orange juice
1½ cups mashed sweet potato
½ cup sultanas
½ cup ground hazelnuts
1 cup self-raising flour, sifted
SPICED CREAM
300 ml carton thickened cream
2 tablespoons golden syrup
1 teaspoon ground ginger
1 teaspoon ground cinnamon
½ teaspoon garam masala

1 Brush a 20 cm springform pan with melted butter or oil. Line the base and sides with paper, then grease the paper. Coat the base and sides with finely ground hazelnuts, shaking off any excess.
2 Beat cream cheese in a small bowl until light and fluffy. Add sugar, rind and eggs. Beat until combined. Transfer mixture to a large mixing bowl.
3 Using a metal spoon, fold in juice, sweet potato, sultanas, hazelnuts and sifted flour until just combined. Pour mixture into the prepared pan and smooth the surface.
4 Bake at 180°C for 1 hour or until a skewer comes out clean when inserted into the centre of the cake. Remove from oven and leave to cool in pan. Refrigerate for several hours or overnight. Serve with Spiced Cream.
5 To make Cream: Combine all ingredients together in a small mixing bowl. Beat until mixture becomes stiff.

Zucchini Apple and Apricot Slice

This delicately flavoured slice is not only healthy but full of fibre also. The tender, cake-like base is complemented by the soft fruity topping.

PREPARATION TIME: *20 minutes +*
10 minutes standing
COOKING TIME: *1 hour*
SERVES 8

125 g butter
½ cup brown sugar
2 egg yolks
1 cup wholemeal self-raising flour
¼ cup wheatgerm
¼ cup finely chopped dried apricots
¼ cup boiling water
425 g can pie-pack apple
1 small zucchini, grated
½ cup rolled oats
½ cup dessicated coconut
2 tablespoons honey
2 egg whites, stiffly beaten

1 Brush a 20 × 30 cm shallow oblong pan with some melted butter or oil. Line the base and sides with greaseproof paper, then grease the paper.
2 Beat butter and sugar in a small bowl with an electric mixer until light and fluffy. Add egg yolks and beat until combined. Using a metal spoon, fold in sifted flour, including husks and wheatgerm. Press mixture over base of prepared pan and smooth the surface.
3 Soak apricots in boiling water for 10 minutes or until apricots are plump and almost all liquid is absorbed.
4 Spread apple over prepared base. Combine undrained apricots with zucchini, oats, coconut and honey in a bowl. Fold in egg whites with a metal spoon.
5 Spoon mixture over apple and smooth the surface. Bake slice at 180°C for 1 hour or until golden and cooked through. Leave slice to cool in pan. Serve with flavoured yoghurt if desired.
Note: Pie-pack apple has been used in this recipe for ease and convenience but if desired freshly cooked apples may be used in place of the canned.

Above: Sweet Potato and Hazelnut Cheesecake. Below: Zucchini, Apple and Apricot Slice. 107

USEFUL INFORMATION

Recipes are all thoroughly tested, using standard metric
measuring cups and spoons. All cup and spoon measurements
are level. We have used eggs with an average weight of 55 g
each in all recipes.

CUP AND SPOON MEASURES

A basic metric cup set consists
of 1 cup, ½ cup, ⅓ cup and
¼ cup sizes. The basic spoon
set comprises 1 tablespoon, 1
teaspoon, ½ teaspoon and ¼
teaspoon.

1 cup	250 mL/8 fl oz
½ cup	125 mL/4 fl oz
⅓ cup	80 mL/
(4 tablespoons)	2½ fl oz
¼ cup	
(3 tablespoons)	60 mL/2 fl oz
1 tablespoon	20 mL
1 teaspoon	5 mL
½ teaspoon	2.5 mL
¼ teaspoon	1.25 mL

DRY MEASURES

Metric	Imperial
15 g	½ oz
30 g	1 oz
45 g	1½ oz
60 g	2 oz
75 g	2½ oz
90 g	3 oz
100 g	3½ oz
125 g	4 oz
155 g	5 oz
170 g	5½ oz
200 g	6½ oz
220 g	7 oz
250 g	8 oz

OVEN TEMPERATURE CHART

	°C	°F	Gas Mark
Very slow	120	250	½
Slow	150	300	1–2
Mod. slow	160	325	3
Moderate	180	350	4
Mod. hot	190	375	5–6
Hot	200	400	6–7

LIQUIDS

Metric	Imperial
30 mL	1 fl oz
60 mL	2 fl oz
100 mL	3½ fl oz
125 mL	4 fl oz
155 mL	5 fl oz
170 mL	5½ fl oz
200 mL	6½ fl oz
220 mL	7 fl oz
250 mL	8 fl oz

THE PUBLISHER THANKS
THE FOLLOWING FOR
THEIR ASSISTANCE IN THE
PHOTOGRAPHY FOR THIS
BOOK:

CORSO DE' FIORI

COUNTRY TRADER

GREGORY FORD ANTIQUES

IN MATERIAL

LIMOGES

MIKASA TABLEWARE

NORITAKE

ROYAL DOULTON

VILLEROY AND BOCH

WATERFORD WEDGWOOD

GLOSSARY

burghul = cracked wheat
butter bean = lima bean
capsicum = sweet pepper
cornflour = cornstarch
cornmeal = polenta
flour = use plain all purpose unless
    otherwise specified
long-grain rice = Carolina rice
pepitas = dried, untoasted pumpkin
    seeds
snow pea = mangetout
tahini paste = tahina paste
zucchini = courgettes

Published by Murdoch Books,
a division of Murdoch Magazines Pty Ltd
213 Miller Street, North Sydney NSW 2060

Murdoch Books Food Editor:
  Jo Anne Calabria
Home Economists: Kerry Carr,
  Voula Manzouridis, Kerrie Ray
Art Direction: Elaine Rushbrooke
Photography: Ray Joyce
Illustrations: James Gordon
Finished Art: Jayne Hunter
Index: Michael Wyatt

Publisher: Anne Wilson
Publishing Manager: Mark Newman
Managing Editor: Sarah Murray
Production Manager: Catie Ziller
Marketing Manager: Mark Smith
National Sales Manager: Keith Watson

Cataloguing-in-Publication Data
Vegetarian cookbook
Includes index.
ISBN 086411 257 2.
1. Vegetarian cookery
641.5636

Printed by Toppan Printing Co. Ltd,
Singapore
Typeset by Post Typesetters, Qld.
© Murdoch Books 1992

Murdoch Books is a trade mark of Murdoch
Magazines Pty Ltd

Distributed in the UK by
Australian Consolidated Press (UK) Ltd,
20 Galowhill Road, Brackmills, Northampton
NN4 0EE Enquiries – 0604 760456

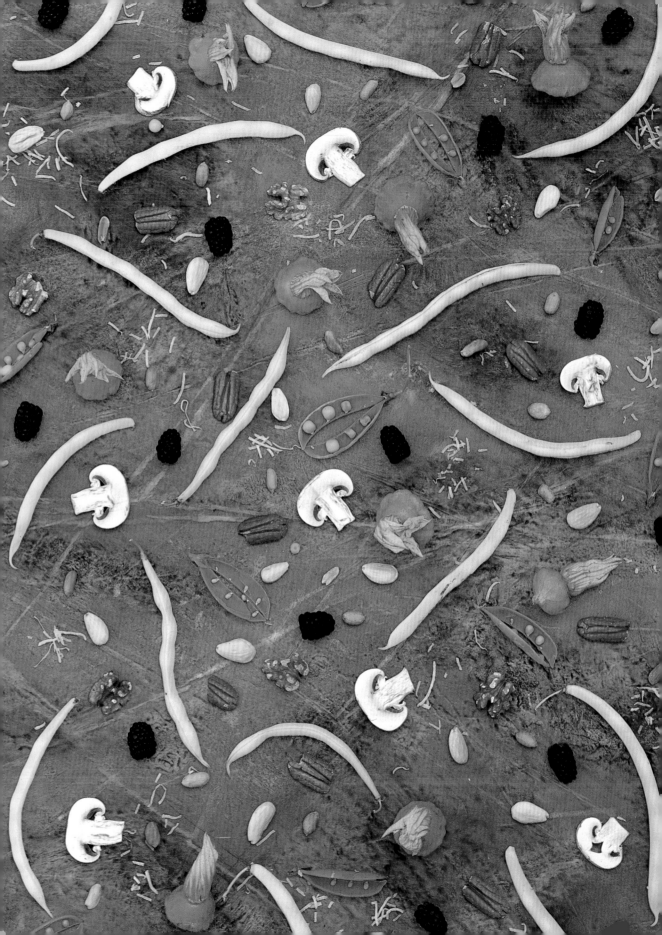